The Same Way

R.A. Smith

Cover Design by Nathan E. Smith

Contents

Introduction

I can think of three predominant reasons, after forty-plus years of ministry, why God has pushed me to put these words in printed form. First and foremost, I have two boys whom I cherish. They have both accompanied me on several occasions when I have led spiritual retreats. They know what I do, and they've heard it. But as I turn sixty this year, I would love to leave something for posterity so that my sons can say, "Here is what my dad was about; this was his life, his passion." I've heard it said that every pastor has only three sermons. If that's true, then these are my three sermons. This is who I am.

The second reason is these thoughts, truths, and reflections that I share on retreats needed to be written down. People will often ask if I have any of this material in printed form. Until now, the answer has been no. It needed to be written so that folks could take these ideas home with them and, hopefully, put them to good use. Every semester I walk through a book with a group of Baylor guys. I pray that one day God will use this book to impact others in the same way.

The third reason is Jesus told me to. No audible voice—just the clear sense to die to myself and follow him. For years now, when I'd feel anxious before speaking to a group, I would go for a short walk and be reminded that it was not me but God who was speaking through me. I'd hold on to this promise—the promise that he would give me the words to say and how to say them. It's a promise he has kept over and over again. This morning I took a walk, and now as I begin to write, I'm reminded of that same promise. And so, with this book, I humbly lay before you my love for my boys, my life and passion in printed form, and my meager obedience to Jesus.

There are a couple of things you need to know before we start. My spiritual journey has shaped this book. My own brokenness and years of ministry drive this endeavor. Those were years spent trying to follow, imitate, and be led by Jesus—and not always very well. I've been at it for forty-five years, and this is as far as I've gotten. It has been a slow transformation, and it has not been pretty. I tell folks that I'm that proverbial guy who works at the drug rehab center. I'm the ex-addict. I'm the ex-ministry addict who's made most all of the mistakes trying to follow Jesus and has made them way too many times. I want to help you find the kind of life that, once you've found it, you sell everything you have in order to obtain it. I'm the beggar who's found more than crumbs and am willing to tell you where I've found them.

The word that best describes the thoughts behind the development of this book is *paradigm*. When I look back over my life, most of the real changes in my walk with Jesus occurred because of what I consider paradigm shifts. Here are some examples. When I was in grade school, I thought Christians were people who went to church and did good. That paradigm changed in the seventh grade. My parents didn't go to church but made sure my sister and I did. When Friendship Baptist Church opened a couple of blocks from our house, it became my new church, strictly based on proximity alone. We could now walk. The second paradigm shift occurred when I found out that, in order to become a Christian in the Baptist church, you had to "walk down the aisle." I had not done that yet and could not think of anything more terrifying. My sister had already performed this heroic act, and now the pressure was on me. To make a long story short, I found a way to trust Christ at a church weekend camp without having to walk the aisle. Now that I had fire insurance and was going to heaven, I assumed everything was done. I was sure there were some finer points to master and some membership obligations to maintain, but the big thing was accomplished, finished, completed. I had arrived and could relax. Little did I know at the age of fourteen that, like most adolescents, my journey had just begun. I had just started something that was going to carry me into eternity.

When I started going to Young Life in high school, I was introduced to another paradigm shift. These folks were talking about a relationship with Jesus. This was earth-shattering. So, the God of the Universe not only died for me but wanted a relationship with me? Wow, that changed everything. In college, I was introduced to the ideas of service, ministry, evangelism, discipleship, etc. And since then, the paradigm shifts just keep coming. They are the course corrections that mark our growth in Christ. Paradigm shifts are the process of the Spirit transforming our minds with the truth.

This book is going to introduce you to several paradigms. You won't work all of these into your life all at once. Jesus will deliver them to you one at a time, and you will grasp them at just the appropriate point in your journey. My hope is to give you a picture of how it all fits.

I want to give you some idea of the larger story and where it leads. But most of all, it's Jesus who wants to take you to a place beyond your wildest dreams.

You will soon find that I have quoted from a small list of authors and only from a singular work of each writer. I have done so on purpose. These are the books that have shaped my life and my soul over the years. I hope that you go out a buy every one of them and that their pages will become marked and tattered from heavy use. I may have been able to find better quotes somewhere else, but what I really want to do is introduce you to my friends. Let me welcome you to my pastor, A.W. Tozer; my professor, Lewis Sperry Chafer; my Quaker friend, Thomas Kelly; my French spiritual director, Jean-Pierre de Caussade; my mentor in humility, Andrew Murray; and a few others we'll meet along the way. Almost all of these thinkers are dead, but their words have stood the test of time, and the books are truly spiritual classics. They have spoken life to me. I hope and pray that you will find and read them and that they will have the same impact on you.

What I have and what I know is this. When Jesus says in John 10:10, "I have come that you might have life, and have it to the full," he is offering life beyond your wildest dreams. I'm dead serious. These aren't just words. You and I have been invited to a life that is truly incomprehensible. I love Jesus' words in the Gospel of John as he invites others into this life. He tells the Samaritan woman at the well that this life is like living water (4:10). If you drink it, you will never thirst again (4:13). That's crazy! Better yet, if you drink it, it will well up inside you to eternal life (4:14). The Fountain of Youth! The Holy Grail! No, it's much better. It's life beyond your wildest dreams. If you hear Jesus' words from a *seen world* perspective, they won't make sense. But, as we'll explore later, Jesus uses *other world* language to invite us into another realm. He invites us to a life beyond our imagination. If this is the life you are already living, then there is no need to read any further. If, however, it is not the life you're living, then, for the next hundred pages or so, I hope Jesus stirs your hunger for something more. I pray he makes you thirsty for something beyond your wildest dreams. I plan to use language from another realm, language that, I hope, will cause you to ponder and wonder. I want to echo some of the convictions that the mystics were burned at the stake for. Assurances that will make you want to live for something outside of yourself. This all may sound a little crazy, but don't stop until the end. Some books start fast and then slowly fade. This one will do just the opposite. It will build gradually, and the last chapter will be the best. I'm praying that your paradigms will be enlarged and that you will find more of Christ than of me in these words. And if you find him, you will have found everything.

1
Holy Name

What's the first thing we see at the beginning of every Star Wars movie? The big opening crawl that delivers essential context for understanding the story we're about to see. It lets us know a little history. It lets us know what's been happening in a "galaxy far, far away." Many times, in order to adequately tell a good story, you need to set the stage. You have to give context, or a person might feel lost in the first scene and be left trying to play catch-up throughout the rest of the story. Or even worse, they might misunderstand some key elements of the plot.

The Scriptures tell a story. It is a great story of redemption. It is the story of God and humans, the creation and the fall, Abraham and the patriarchs, of Moses and the law, the journey of Israel and the coming of Jesus, and of our salvation. In the Scriptures, there is a promise of life and a promise for a future. It is a GREAT story. It is a story that God and Jesus sit in the middle of, and yet in many ways it is our story as well. But I'm not sure it is the story. I'm not sure it's even God's story in the full sense of the word. I think God's story is bigger. The Scriptures—as recorded in Genesis through Revelation—tell the story of our humanity but seem to allude to a larger story, without ever coming out and giving us all the details. They give us just enough to conclude that the larger story exists. And that this larger story, if we could comprehend it, would be an incredible aid to understanding our own story. It would tell us how we fit. It would explain some of the whys. This larger story would provide some measure of context for us and the small stories that we live out each day. I'd like to point out that God has revealed to me neither the larger story nor its context on magic stone tablets. But, he has been sending us clues, bread crumbs, all along the way in order that we might catch a glimpse, a perception of this larger story.

Before I invite you to the Scriptures, let me show you a small picture of this notion. In 1876, George Mc-Donald, a Scottish pastor and writer, wrote a book of fiction about a young curate—a rookie priest—who finds an unlikely mentor in a local gatekeeper, a dwarf named Polwarth. What follows are parts of two conversations between Polwarth and the inexperienced curate. Remember, this is just a picture, an analogy. Polwarth starts:

> "Let me just ask you a question, to make the nature of what I say clear to you: Tell me, if you can, what primarily did Jesus, from his own account of himself, come into the world to do?"
> "To save it," answered Wingfold readily.
> "I think you are wrong," returned Polwarth. "Mind, I said primarily. I think you will come to the same conclusion yourself by and by. An honest man will never ultimately fail to get at what Jesus means if he studies Jesus' life and teachings long enough. I have seen him described somewhere as a man dominated by the passion of humanity—or something like that. But, another passion was the light of his life, and dominated even that which would yet have been enough to make him lay down his life." [1]

So, what is the primary reason Christ came into the world? This is a fundamental question that every believer should be able to answer. What was the passion that dominated his life? The question takes us to the main theme of the larger story, and the answer to the question lies at the center of the plot.

If we looked just at our smaller, human story, we might be tempted to believe that the larger story is about us. We'd be tempted to believe that we sit in the center of the story and that Jesus came to save us. This was the curate's first inclination. (A small note here: Don't you love the fact that Polwarth doesn't answer his own question. He lets the curate discover it on his own. And when Wingfold does eventually discover it, it will be ten times more powerful. The impact will be life-changing.) The next conversation between Polwarth and Wingfold takes place sometime later, further along in the curate's journey with Christ.

> One evening the curate went earlier than usual and had tea with the Polwarths.
> "Do you remember," he asked of his host, "once putting the question to me, what our Lord came into this world for?"
> "I do," answered Polwarth.
> "And you remember I answered you wrong: I said it was to save the world?"
> "Yes, just so you put it."
> "Well, I think I can answer the question correctly now; and in learning the true answer I have learned much. Did he not come first of all to do the will of his Father? Was not his Father first with him always and his fellowmen next; for they were his Father's?"
> "I need hardly say it at this point—for you know you are right. Jesus is ten times more real a person to you, is he not, since you discovered that truth?" [2]

Something has happened to the curate—a paradigm shift in his mind, an awakening in his soul. The story has been

11

enlarged. We humans are no longer the center of the story; God is. Jesus' obedience to the Father sits close to that center, and the story has become about God. Now we are on the verge of true and real context.

Within the Scriptures, I think we find the clearest delivery of the "big picture" in Ezekiel 36 and the new covenant between God and His people. I like it because it comes roughly 550 years before the birth of Christ. It gives us an Old Testament look at what God was about to do with the coming of the Messiah. It puts the good news of the gospel of Jesus into context. The redemptive work of Christ literally flows out of what God is doing in the history of the Old Testament and the journey of Israel. Let me set the stage.

The Old Testament is full of accounts of Israel's inability to keep the law, despite God's promised judgment in Deuteronomy. In 722 BC, God used the Assyrians to carry out this judgment. They came down and defeated the northern kingdom of Israel and carried off the survivors as slaves. The southern kingdom of Judah was spared only by the reluctant faith of King Hezekiah (Isa. 36, 37). However, Judah continued to be disobedient, and in 605 BC the prophet Daniel and others began to be subjugated and were brought to Babylon by King Nebuchadnezzar. In 586 BC God finally judged Judah and Jerusalem; the city and the temple were destroyed, and most of the remaining Israelites were taken to Babylon into captivity. It is in this captivity that Ezekiel prophesies to the nation Israel while they are enslaved. This could be the lowest point in Israel's history. The Israelites are exiled and without hope. For most of the book, Ezekiel expounds on their sin, the sin of other nations and the many reasons they are being disciplined by God.

Then in Chapter 36, Ezekiel gives hope to the people of Israel. In essence, God says, "Here's what I'm about to do, and it is good news."

> Therefore say to the house of Israel, "This is what the Sovereign Lord says: It is not for your sake, O house of Israel, that I am going to do these things, but for the sake of my holy name, which you have profaned among the nations where you have gone." (Ezek. 36:22)

Stop and pause right here. Do not miss this. God is about to do something amazing. It is something that will culminate in the coming of the Messiah, Jesus. And God is going to do this, why? Because of his great love for his chosen people Israel? NO! Because of his incomprehensible love for the church to come? NO! Because of his crazy, passionate love for you and me? NO! He is doing it because of his "*Holy Name.*" A name that has been "profaned among the nations."

Here is the heart of God. Here is insight into what motivates God to do what he does. His holy name is the theme of the larger story. I'm not saying God doesn't love us. He does. Scripture declares it over and over again. But I am saying that there was a reason he loved us, and you and I don't sit in the center of that reason. God's concern for his holy name is a significant piece of the larger story and is part of why he's chosen to love us. This revelation clearly shows that it's a story in which you and I don't sit in the center. Israel is not the center of this story. The Church is not the center. The small stories that we live out each day are not the center. God's holy name, and his regard for it, sits in the center and drives the story. I have to confess that, when I hear this, I'm relieved. There is a part of our souls that knows we were not made for the responsibility of driving the larger story, and it longs to hear that there is someone else who is.

The next verse is what I believe to be the shortest, most succinct description in all of Scripture of the big picture of what God is doing. God tells the nation Israel, and us, "The nations will know that I am the Lord, declares the Sovereign Lord, when I show myself holy through you before their eyes" (Ezek. 36:23; italics mine). This is what God is doing. This is the larger story.

First, he is going to "show [himself] holy." Another translations says, "make my name holy." This is the key to the plot of the larger story. If someone were to ask, what is God doing in the world today, this is the answer: God is making his name holy. Something must have occurred to call into question God's name, his character, and who he is. And God is in the process of answering those questions. Showing himself holy is what he is doing, and it's the primary reason Jesus came. Are you surprised? Does it rattle your paradigms? Let's keep going.

The second part is where you and I, the Church, and Israel fit in. Jesus, though not yet named, is going to have the starring role. He will be in the center of all the action and will be the hero in the fullest sense. You and I also have a role to play, and it is front and center. God has chosen to put us right in the middle of the drama. He is going to show himself holy "through you." That's right, we play a major supporting role in the great drama that God is writing, producing, and directing. It is a huge privilege that he has chosen to include us. We didn't earn it. We were selected on the basis of grace. But it is a significant role nonetheless. And it is our destiny. It is why we have been selected.

The last element of the great play is connected to

who is watching. God is making his name holy—through you—"before their eyes." These "eyes," in the immediate context, indicates "the nations" referenced earlier in the passage. God promises to make his name holy through Israel before all these nations. There is a future aspect to this pledge that has yet to be fulfilled, an aspect that impacts you and me and all believers.

It carries itself all the way into the New Testament and into our day. The life of Christ is a testament to all nations, and every knee will ultimately bow (Phil. 2:9-11). You and I and all the believers before us have been lights, which "shine like stars in the universe" among crooked and depraved generations (Phil. 2:14-17). When Jesus teaches us to pray The Lord's Prayer, he starts with what should be the thought that drives and motivates our lives: "hallowed be Thy name." If the passion that stirs God's heart is the same passion that compels ours, we will be used by him to be a shining testament to God's holy name. We have been included in a great story, an amazing drama.

However, it gets even bigger. We have talked about "their eyes" from a seen world perspective but not from an unseen world perspective. God is going to do something "through you" not only before the eyes of the nations but before even the eyes of the angels. The story is bigger than you can imagine! God is redeeming us, and he's doing it in front of angels and demons. Everyone is watching. Nothing is hidden. When we sin in our secret closets, thinking no one is watching, no one is being hurt, we are mistaken. Everything is out in the open. Every moment counts. Paul says, "[God's] intent was that now through the church the manifold wisdom of God should be made known to rulers and authorities [demons] in

15

the heavenly realms, according to his eternal purpose which he accomplished in Christ Jesus our Lord" (Eph. 3:10-11). In other words, God's story is being played out before a celestial audience. Welcome to the larger story. Welcome to context. And we are still not finished.

I've saved the best for last. Returning to the passage, we notice that God is going to "show myself holy, through you, before their eyes" (Ezek. 36:23; italics mine). Did you notice who's doing the work? God is going to make his name holy. He's not asking for help. It's all on him. And did you notice, when it comes to being included and having a role, God is going to do his work "through" you? You are not being asked to initiate the work, nor to finish what he's started. God is going to perform it, and he's going to do so utilizing you. Let's take a quick look at the verses that follow:

> For I will take you out of the nations; I will gather you from all the countries and bring you back into your land. I will sprinkle clean water on you, and you will be clean; I will cleanse you from all your impurities and from all your idols. I will give you a new heart and put a new spirit in you; I will remove from you your heart of stone and give you a heart of flesh. And I will put my Spirit in you and move you to follow my decrees and be careful to keep my laws. You will live in the land I gave your forefathers; you will be my people, and I will be your God. I will save you from all your uncleanness. (Ezek. 36:24-29)

These verses describe the process of how God is going to use our lives to make his name holy. Notice the two words that are repeated over and over again. What are they? __ _____. It is God who is going to do all the work, and he is going to do it "through" us. This is what is called an unconditional covenant. Its fulfillment rests entirely on the shoulders of God. This is a radically different paradigm than the one we Christians typically operate under. There is nothing to be earned—only an invitation to be included in what God is doing. It is an invitation to life beyond our wildest dreams.

Here is a reminder: it has always been on his shoulders. God has always been working for the sake of his name. Everything that we have ever done has been a response to something he has already initiated. This has been the platform from the beginning. God led the nation of Israel out of Egypt, and the people followed. God spoke through the prophets, and Israel failed to listen. Christ came and died on the cross, and we respond in faith. We love because he first loved us (1 John 4:19). This is the fundamental rhythm of life in God and Christ.

A.W. Tozer speaks of this rhythm in *The Pursuit of God*:

> Christian theology teaches the doctrine of prevenient grace, which briefly stated means this, that before a man can seek God, God must first have sought man. Before a sinful man can think a right thought of God, there must have been a work of enlightenment done within him; imperfect it may be, but a true work nonetheless, and the secret cause of all desiring and seeking and praying may follow. We pursue God because, and only because, He has first put an urge within us that spurs us to the pursuit. "No man can come to me," said the Lord, "except the Father which hath sent me draw him," and it is by this very prevenient drawing that God takes from us every vestige of credit for the act of coming. The impulse to pursue God originates with God, but the outworking of that impulse is our following hard after Him; and all the time we are pursuing Him we are already in His hand: "Thy right hand upholdeth me." In this divine "upholding" and human "following" there is no contra-

diction. All is of God, for as von Hugel teaches, God is always previous. [3]

Eugene H. Peterson in *Working the Angles* sees this same principle in prayer:

> The appearances mislead: prayer is never the first word, it is always the second word. God has the first word. Prayer is answering speech; it is not primarily "address" but "response." Essential to the practice of prayer is to fully realize this secondary quality… Prayer is a human word and is never the first word, never the primary word, never the initiating and shaping word simply because we are never first, never primary. [4]

This idea that God is always previous, always leading, always inviting, is a fundamental piece of the larger story. Paul tells the church in Corinth, "Thanks be to God, who always leads us in triumphal procession in Christ and through us spreads everywhere the fragrance of the knowledge of him" (2 Cor. 2:14). He always leads; we respond. God is doing something. He is doing something for the sake of his holy name. He sits in the center of the larger story. He is inviting you and me into that story. And it's a life beyond our wildest dreams.

2
The Battle

Our souls are intrigued by the thought of a larger story. Let me ask a question: How did the story start? If someone were to ask you when your story began, how would you answer? Would you take us back to your birth, the day it all began? Or would you take us back to the moment you trusted Christ, the day you decided to follow Jesus? There may not be a specific day. Is there another time, another moment? We tend to see things through the lens of our own eyes and the seen world we live in. But what if you were to ask God this question about your story and when it began? How would he answer? God's answer might surprise us. He would say our story started long before we were born. "For he chose us in him before the creation of the world to be holy and blameless in his sight" (Eph. 1:4). Somehow God knew us and initiated with us before the foundation of the earth.

Assuming our story fits into the larger story, when did this larger story start? When did the drama that the Lord is writing, producing, and directing begin? Our answers here can vary. Most of us will probably go to Genesis 1: "In the beginning." We assume that's when everything started. And it's true in some ways, but it's a seen world answer. Others will say that, due to the eternal nature of God, the Alpha and the Omega, there is no beginning. And that would be correct and theologically accurate. But every story, every drama has to have a beginning somewhere in time. So, when did the story of God's concern for his holy name start? Of course, there's no definitive answer, such as 5000 BC. I ask the question for this reason: I want to move us beyond the seen world answer, for there lies context.

With that in mind, if we're looking for context to the larger story, then what happened before "In the beginning"? Again, we don't know a lot, but the Bible does give us some clues. Before the creation of the universe, God existed. The Father, the Son, and the Holy Spirit enjoyed one another. There was relationship. But was there anything else? What was the first thing God created? Good question. Again, no definitive answer, but we do have clues. When Isaiah and John each are lifted up and brought before the throne of God in a vision, there are creatures hovering above the Lord singing, "Holy, Holy, Holy is the Lord God Almighty" (Isa. 6:3; Rev. 4:8). And they sing it day and night. We could deduce that they have been singing it, almost forever. But they are not eternal beings, so they had to be created. I think, before "In the beginning," God created angels. This is context to the larger story.

Here is a little of what we know about angels. It, of course, is not a complete theological summary, but we know they are messengers or servants of God—think of Gabriel's message to Mary (Luke 1:28). We know that, when humans first meet or are confronted by angels, our natural response is fear; we fall on our knees—consider the shepherds at the birth of Jesus (Luke 2:8-9) or Balaam and his donkey (Num. 22:31). We know they are so much more powerful than humans—one (that's right, one!) an-

20

gel kills 185,000 Assyrians in a single night (Isa. 37:36). We know there's no record of God ever indwelling an angel or uniting himself to one. And we know there was an angel named Lucifer, who set himself up to be equal to the Most High God (Isa. 14:12-14). He was cast out of heaven and down to earth. He is known to us as the devil. His pride is the root of all evil. There was a rebellion and other angels joined Lucifer and are now known as demons. I will refer to the devil and his fellow demons as the enemy. They are not like God. They are created beings. They are not all-knowing, all-powerful, nor ever-present. They are not God.

The ensuing battle between God and the enemy, between the good angels and the bad, is one of the most significant pieces of context for the larger story, and it speaks to how we should live our lives each day. There's been a battle between good and evil going on long before Genesis 3, when the serpent approached Adam and Eve. This battle is so significant that it is somehow ingrained into our souls and psyches. Think about this. All the great stories that have ever been written have this as their central theme. The battle between good and evil drives the plot of The Lord of the Rings, Star Wars, Harry Potter, and… And this is just our era. All stories seem to have this theme somewhere in the center of their plot. The idea of redemption—that good triumphs over evil—is imbedded in the core of who we are as humans. I don't know what the timeline looks like and where Genesis 1 fits into the fall of the angels, but you almost get the sense that we were made for this battle. Regardless of the exact timeline and when certain events occurred, God in his sovereign omniscience knew what was coming and made us uniquely suited for this war. Here is the important thing to take away. One of the most significant pieces of context to our understanding of the larger story is that it is being played out in a cosmic battle between good and evil, between God and the enemy. This should cause a huge paradigm shift for us.

It certainly has for me. I became a believer in 1972 at Glen Rose Baptist Encampment (sounds like a prison, doesn't it?). A cheerleader named Vickie was supposed to be on that trip, and her potential presence was my main motivation for being there. That first night, after the message, as we were all going to bed, our leader said that, if anyone had questions or wanted to talk, he would be available. I thought, here's my chance to meet Jesus and not have to "walk down the aisle." So, after I thought everyone was asleep, the leader prayed with me, and that night I became a Christian in a dormitory bathroom. As it turns out, Vickie had canceled and didn't come, and I met Jesus. My life and my destiny have never been the same. I love to tell that story.

But—and it's a big but—no one told me that night that I was entering into a war. No one told me that, when I trusted Jesus for the forgiveness of my sins, I had joined sides in a cosmic battle. No one told me that there were unseen beings who were incredibly powerful and who had now become my enemy. No one told me that this enemy was like an angry lion out to kill, steal, and destroy (1 Peter 5:8; John 10:10). I was in no way prepared for that fight. And it showed. I was a pretty good kid until I became a Christian. But the middle years of my adolescence were, for me, nothing but carnage from a losing battle. My parents divorced that summer, the alcoholic genes from my father's side of the family struck regularly, and I was angry, hurt, and lost. Yes, I was a believer. I had trusted Christ. But I had no idea how I fit into the larger story. I barely knew one existed. I'd met Jesus, but I was still somewhat lost. The Scriptures talk about certain people being lost. These lost folks stand outside the wall and are considered excluded from the family of God. I think there is a degree of lostness for those inside the family as well. This lostness is determined by how well they are connected to the larger story, and I was definitely not connected. I was in, but I was lost.

Slowly, over the years, I heard rumors of this battle. In seminary we talked about the theological nature, but not necessarily the realities, of demons and the war. I think I can say that the idea of training for a genuine, undeniable battle against the enemy was foreign to me. It was talked about, referred to, but the battle had no actual sense of being a reality. The actuality of it rarely touched my day-to-day life. And yet awareness of this battle is absolutely crucial to living life in the larger story. It may be the most practical piece of context. Personally, this concept of a daily battle is something I have struggled with. It's like I know it to be true, but my life and actions say that I don't believe it.

I'm an optimist, so my cup is usually more than half full. My denial of the other half of reality has caused me to live most of my days oblivious to the idea of spiritual battle. Picture, if you will, a war movie. In this scene the enemy is close, everywhere, hiding in the brush. The lead character, though, is strolling down a trail through the jungle, wearing florescent colors. His weapon is strapped on his back and not accessible. He has headphones on and is singing along to Led Zeppelin's "Stairway to Heaven" as loudly as he can. It appears that he doesn't have a care in the world and life is good. He's acting like the enemy doesn't even exist. Well, that was me on most days, and it's still where I have a tendency to drift. If we are not cognizant of the fact that the enemy exists, how easy is it going to be for him to attack us? Awareness of the battle is the most practical piece of context to our daily lives.

The Scriptures warn us not only to be aware of the battle but also to be prepared for it. In Ephesians 6, Paul says that the battle is not against flesh and blood and that we are to put on the full armor of God. We hear sermons admonishing us to gird our loins with truth, to put on the breast plate of righteousness, the shoes of readiness, the shield of faith, the helmet of salvation, and the sword of the Spirit, which is the word of God. I have nothing much to add other than the reminder that this is something we are to do every day. The battle is all day long, and all night as well. It is real.

But if this is really God's fight, if he's the one who's going to "show himself holy," what is our part? Notice the kind of intentionality he's inviting us to in Ephesians 6:10-17.

> Finally, be strong in the Lord and in his mighty power. Put on the full armor of God so that you can take your stand against the devil's schemes. For our struggle is not against flesh and blood, but against the rulers, against the authorities, against the powers of this dark world, against the spiritual forces of evil in the heavenly realms. Therefore put on the full armor of God, so that when the day of evil comes, you may be able to stand your ground, and after you have done everything, to stand. Stand firm then, with the belt of truth buckled around your waist, with the breastplate of righteousness in place, and with your feet fitted with the readiness

that comes from the gospel of peace. In addition
to all this, take up the shield of faith, with which
you can extinguish all the flaming arrows of the evil
one. Take the helmet of salvation and the sword of
the Spirit, which is the word of God.

The language instructs you not to attack but to stand
your ground. Do not let the enemy move you. We do this
by "putting on armor." It is language Paul has used before
when he encourages his readers to "clothe yourselves"
(Rom. 13:14; Col. 3:12). This idea is consistent with Paul's
exhortation to "put off the old man" and to "put on the
new man" (Eph. 4:22-24). All of this is connected to what
we believe. The way we stand ready in battle is by believing that all of what we have put on—the armor—is true.
We trust it. And when we do, God invites us into the battle with the following emphasis.

And pray in the Spirit on all occasions with all
kinds of prayers and requests. With this in mind, be
on the alert, always keep praying for all the saints.
Pray also for me, that whenever I open my mouth,
words may be given to me so that I will fearlessly
make known the mystery of the gospel, for which
I am an ambassador in chains. Pray that I may de-
clare it fearlessly, as I should. (Eph. 6:18-20)

There is one word, one idea, one concept, one action, that
is repeated five times in these three verses: prayer. Prayer
is our response, our intentionality. Prayer is how God invites you and me to engage in the battle.

There's one other thing I want to remind us of in
terms of this battle. We tend to see it from a seen world
perspective—drugs, sex, and rock and roll. But these are
just the outer layers of a deeper issue. The enemy sees sin
for what it is and will attack with this thought in mind.

In Luke 4, when Jesus is led into the wilderness for forty days and nights, the enemy comes to tempt him. Notice the nature of the three temptations. The first temptation is, "If you are the Son of God tell these stones to become bread." On a human level, Satan is attacking Jesus' body and its need for food. But on a much deeper level, he is attacking Jesus' central purpose. The enemy seems, on the surface, to question Jesus on whether he is the Son of God. The devil knows he is the Son of God from ages past, and Jesus knows it too. His Father had recently confirmed it again at his baptism (Luke 3:22). Ultimately, the temptation is not a question of identity, and certainly not one of food, but of dependence. Would Jesus trust the Father to take care of him, feed him, and give him just what he needed? The key element in Jesus' coming was that he came to defeat the enemy. He would do that by taking bodily form and living a perfect life of trust, wholly dependent on the Father. This dependence is the root of humility. Andrew Murray says this in his book *Humility*:

> Hence it follows that nothing can be our redemption but the restoration of the lost humility, the original and only true relation of the creature to its God. And so Jesus came to bring humility back to earth, to make us partakers of it, and by it to save us. In heaven He humbled Himself to become man. The humility we see in Him possessed Him in heaven; it brought Him, He brought it, from there. Here on earth "He humbled Himself, and became obedient unto death"; His humility gave His death its value, and so became our redemption. And now the salvation He imparts is nothing less and nothing else than a communication of His own life and death, His own disposition and spirit—His own humility—as the ground and root of His relation to God and His redeeming work. Jesus Christ took the place and fulfilled the destiny of man,

as creature, by His life of perfect humility. His humility is our salvation. His salvation is our humility. [1]

The other two temptations follow the same thought. This is my paraphrase of the enemy's next attack: "Jesus, you can have it now, I'll give you all of it, just trust me instead of the Father." And in the last temptation, he counters with, "Jesus, if you are God, on the basis of the promise of Scripture, initiate, lead, do something on your own, instead of being dependent on the leading of your Father." Jesus, of course, answered wisely on all accounts. The humility of dependence wins the day. When the enemy comes after us, he will attack in the same way. He will tempt us to put our trust and dependence in something or someone other than God. It may seem like the attacks are all about the cravings of sinful man—the lust of his eyes, the pride of life—but underneath, it will be about what we trust and depend on. It has been the same attack, the same lie from the very beginning.

I'll close with a reminder that context is the key. The enemy wants us to think that he doesn't exist and that sin is just dirt. And if we buy those lies, then surely there is something we can do to clean ourselves up and remedy the problem by ourselves. But let me communicate the goodness of the gospel in the context of war. We were not just dirtied by sin; we were captured by the enemy. Sin had so entangled our hearts that we had become willing slaves to Satan, the god of this world, and we didn't even know it. Christ, the warrior, comes to this earth to do battle for us. He comes to win us back. At times, as the warrior, Jesus is almost incognito. People hardly knew the King was here, but every once in a while, he would flash his sword. In Revelation 19:15, when Jesus returns, arriving on the clouds and riding a white horse, John records that "out of his mouth comes a sharp sword" with which he does battle. In 2 Thessalonians 2:8, Paul says that, when the lawless one is revealed, Jesus will overthrow him with "the breath of his mouth." These verses both allude to the fact that, in the end, Jesus will defeat the enemy with words, using the same voice that spoke heaven and earth into being. So, when Jesus heals at a distance with just a word, he flashes his sword. When Jesus stands in the front of a boat and commands the wind and waves to "be still," he flashes his sword, and the disciples are speechless.

Even as Jesus walks toward the cross, the enemy thinks evil is winning. The enemy's own pride blinds him. At the cross, Jesus washes away our sin with his blood, and with his death, he sets us free from our captivity. Free at last! And with his resurrection, we become new creations. God defeats pride with humility. All this is ours, by faith, if we trust it. But consider carefully. Because whenever we decide to trust Jesus and follow him out of our old captivity, we in essence have chosen sides in the great cosmic battle between good and evil. We now have an enemy. It's our choice. We either remain slaves on the side of the enemy, or we become free people, redeemed, bought at a price, but still in the midst of a battle. Keep in mind, in this war between good and evil, between God and the enemy, there is no Switzerland, no neutral ground, just two sides.

3
Unseen

Now is as good time as any to introduce an illustration that I think will be helpful moving forward. I was told that all the great spiritual classics have illustrations, and I should also be sensitive to visual learners. So, welcome to my pyramid. I'm a math person, so we are stuck with a geometric figure. The pyramid represents the larger story, or the life that Jesus invites us to.

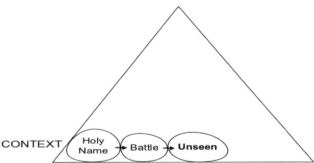

Notice, we are starting at the bottom, laying a foundation. These four sections, or stones, on the bottom represent context. Without the foundation of context, it will be hard to understand the true nature of the life that Jesus is inviting us to and how he plans to deliver it. In the following chapters, we will talk more about this life, which is further up the pyramid. Chapter 1, Holy Name,

29

reminds us that God is in the process of making his name holy, and that endeavor is what drives the larger story. It is the theme and the starting point. In Chapter 2, we unveiled the Battle and explored how it adds context to the story and how it impacts the way we live. It also starts to explain how God's name has been questioned. It helps us understand the significance of why God is "making his name holy." The stones of this foundation of context will build and connect with each other from left to right as we go along. The context of the story will seem to unfold.

In the previous chapter, we were awakened to the reality of angels and the enemy and to a battle we can't see. This takes us to the next stone in our foundation, the concept of the Unseen. It is so simple and yet so profound that we tend to miss it. We wake up every morning in a world we can see. We tend to see, think, and live life from a seen world perspective. It's assumed by most that this seen world is the only one that exists. Others, who might believe in the existence of an unseen realm, usually don't believe the realm is real in the same sense as the seen. For them, the unseen realm tends to be almost magical. But all of this thinking—disregarding or misjudging the unseen world—is a product of sin and the fall. The enemy wants us to believe that evil is neither present nor real, that it doesn't exist. But to deny the unseen realm is to live in darkness, which is precisely where the enemy wants to keep us. The Scriptures, on the other hand, are constantly reminding us that there is another realm, an unseen one, which coexists with the seen. And it is most definitely real.

In the Old Testament, Elisha the prophet was surrounded by the King of Aram in the city of Dothan.

When the servant of the man of God got up and

wentout early the next morning, an army with horses and chariots had surrounded the city. "Oh, my lord, what shall we do?" the servant asked. "Don't be afraid," the prophet answered. "Those who are with us are more than those who are with them." And Elisha prayed, "O Lord, open his eyes so he may see." Then the Lord opened the servant's eyes, and he looked and saw the hills full of horses and chariots of fire all around Elisha. (2 Kings 6:15-17) It is the Spirit of God who gives us eyes to see. When we trusted Jesus for the first time and entered into a covenant relationship with him, we entered into the unseen realm, where God lives. As Christians, every time we trust God or pray to him, we are bumping up against, entering, and participating in the unseen realm. And it's a realm that is certain and true and a realm that Jesus invites us to.

The books of Matthew and Mark tell us that, when Jesus came on the scene, his first sermons touched on the same message. He told listeners, "Repent, for the kingdom is near" (Matt. 4:17, Mark 1:15). Some translations use the phrase "at hand" to describe the kingdom of God. Multiple volumes have been written on the kingdom of God, and it's clear by the size of the book you hold in your hand that that's not the purpose of this one. I want to stay focused on the context of the larger story. The takeaway for us is that the kingdom was "near." It was fast approaching. In fact, because Jesus, the King, was standing right there in front of them, the kingdom was so close, so "at hand," that it was just beyond their fingertips. Extend your arm. All the way as far as you can. Right there, just beyond your reach, there's the kingdom, but you can't see it. It's near. It's right here in the room, but it's unseen.

Jesus tells the Pharisees, "The kingdom of God does not come with your careful observation, nor will people say, 'Here it is,' or 'There it is,' because the kingdom of God is within you" (Luke 17:20-21). In other words, it is not perceived like the seen world is. It has an unseen world quality to it. In each of the synoptic gospels, what follows Jesus' first sermon is the casting out of demons. The authors of the gospels are telling us that the kingdom of God, this unseen realm, is right here. Jesus talked about it, and then he showed it to us, but we still couldn't see it. "But if I drive out demons by the finger of God, then the kingdom of God has come to you" (Luke 11:20). The key point is that Jesus is not just showing us; he is also inviting us to the unseen realm. He's inviting you and me right now, to come.

He's not asking us to leave nor neglect the seen world, but he is saying the unseen trumps the seen. Let me see if I can explain this better. The unseen world permeates the seen. We should be in both at the same time. Jesus was the master of being present in both worlds simultaneously, as we'll see later. This dual-realm existence seems to be outside the norm of everything we know. All we have known is one realm. We were born into the seen, we've grown up in the seen, and it is what we know best. We didn't know anything else existed.

But when we trust Christ and become believers, our eyes are opened, and we are introduced to the unseen in so many different facets. The actual act of trusting Christ's finished work on the cross requires us not only to perceive but to believe things we couldn't see before. The essence of faith is an experience of and a belief in unseen realities. The act of prayer is an unseen reality. The indwelling of the Spirit is an unseen reality. Almost everything we do that is considered spiritual is connected to the unseen realm. The word "spirit" itself literally means "without body" and is born out of the unseen realm.

In fact, we enter the Christian life with a movement from death to life, from darkness to light. It is a movement from earth towards heaven, from the enemy toward God; a movement from blindness to sight, from the seen to the unseen.

> I am sending you to them to open their eyes and turn them from darkness to light, and from the power of Satan to God. (Acts 26:17-18)
>
> As for you, you were dead in your transgressions and sins, in which you used to live when you followed the ways of this world and of the ruler of the kingdom of the air, the spirit who is now at work in those who are disobedient. All of us also lived among them at one time, gratifying the cravings of our sinful nature and following its desires and thoughts. Like the rest, we were by nature objects of wrath. But because of his great love for us, God, who is rich in mercy, made us alive with Christ even when we were dead in transgressions…
> (Eph. 2:1-5)

These passages reference the unseen realities of the work of God. They speak of the movement of redemption—from darkness to light, death to life, from the seen to the unseen. The enemy is referred to as the "god of this age/world" (2 Cor. 4:4). This seen world is his domain. When you become a Christian, your citizenship is transferred from this world, the seen world, to heaven, the unseen (Phil. 3:20). Which of the two worlds is dominant, which will last the longest? It is the larger world, the unseen. If asked, Jesus would refer to the unseen realm as the "real world." You and I think just the opposite, to our demise.

I love how John in his gospel shows Jesus inviting us to the unseen. In Chapter 1, upon meeting Simon, Jesus gives him a new name, Peter (Rock)—an unseen, but later to be experienced, reality. In Chapter 2, in the temple, Jesus tells the Jewish leaders, "Destroy this temple and I will raise it in three days." He was, of course, referring to his body and the resurrection, and not the seen temple they were standing in. In Chapter 3, Jesus tells Nicodemus, "I tell you the truth, no one can enter the kingdom of God unless he is born of water and Spirit." Again, he is referring to our spiritual birth, an unseen reality. In Chapter 4, Jesus speaks to the woman at the well about living water and says, "Whoever drinks the water I give him will never thirst, the water I give him will become in him a spring of water welling up to eternal life" (John 4:14). This is clearly not a seen world reality but an invitation to something beyond what we can imagine.

In Chapter 6, Jesus says, "I am the bread of life. He who comes to me will never go hungry and he who believes in me will never be thirsty" (John 6:35). He goes on to say, "Unless you eat the flesh of the Son of Man and drink his blood, you have no life in you" (John 6:53). None of these are seen world realities but invitations to life in the unseen. In Chapter 7, Jesus says, "I am with you only for a short time, and then I go to the one who sent me. You will look for me, but you will not find me; and where I am, you cannot come" (John 7:33-34). Heaven, where Jesus and the Father are, is in the unseen realm. In Chapter 8, the one who testifies on Jesus' behalf is his Father, who can't be seen. Later in that chapter, Jesus affirms, "Before Abraham was born, I am" (John 8:58). It is one of seven "I am" statements in which he claims to be the unseen, preexistent God. In Chapter 9, he professes, "While I am in the world, I am the light of the world" (John 9:5). This is another unseen reality. And after healing a man born blind, Jesus says to him, "For judgment I have come into the world, so that the blind will see and those who see will become blind" (John 9:39). Again, he is talking about spiritual blindness, an unseen blindness.

In Chapter 10, Jesus is the gate and the good shepherd, both unseen realities. Later in Chapter 10, he tells the Jews, "Believe the miracles, that you may know and understand that the Father is in me, and I in the Father" (John 10:38). The miracles were seen, but the union of Father and Son, the basis of the Trinity, is an unseen reality. In Chapter 11, Jesus tells the disciples, "Our friend Lazarus has fallen asleep; but I am going there to wake him up" (John 11:11). Why would Jesus continue to talk in this language of the unseen with the disciples? It was confusing for them. Their seen world lens was the only way they knew to perceive things. It's because he's subtly inviting them, just as he is inviting you and me, into the unseen realm. In Chapter 12, Jesus tells the world,
You are going to have the light just a little while longer. Walk while you have the light, before darkness overtakes you. The man who walks in the dark does not know where he is going. Put your trust in the light while you have it, so that you may become sons of light. (John 12:35-36)

The invitation is to you and me: enter into the unseen realm and become "sons of light." The only way we can experience Jesus is through faith, by bringing the unseen world into the seen. The only way the invisible Spirit can lead us is if we bring the unseen world into the seen. And the Father, who is spirit, who is unseen, invites us to bring the unseen into the seen. It is our only source of real life. And it is life beyond our wildest seen world dreams.

This is not some novel idea. I'm not the first one to talk like this. For centuries the saints have proclaimed this, just not always in terms of seen and unseen. Typically, they spoke of the kingdom of heaven. They talked about having an eternal perspective. They tried to keep their focus on spiritual, unseen things. A.W. Tozer speaks of this:

> Our trouble is that we have established bad thought habits. We habitually think of the visible world as real and doubt the reality of any other. We do not deny the existence of the spiritual world but we doubt that it is real in the accepted meaning of the word. The world of sense intrudes upon our attention day and night for the whole of our life time. It is clamorous, insistent and self-demonstrating. It does not appeal to our faith; it is here, assaulting our five senses, demanding to be accepted as real and final. But sin has so clouded the lenses of our hearts that we cannot see that other reality, the City of God, shining around us. The world of sense triumphs. The visible becomes the enemy of the invisible; the temporal, of the eternal. This is the curse inherited by every member of Adam's tragic race.[1]

Nothing has changed; the saints, Tozer, all talk of a different realm. My soul, my new heart, is attracted to the unseen realm and longs for it. The great stories of our era invite us here. They invite us to a galaxy far, far away. J.R.R. Tolkien invites us to "middle earth" to fight that which is evil. C.S. Lewis invites us to adventures through a wardrobe and into Narnia with Aslan. J. K. Rowling invites us to Hogwarts. We were made for this other realm, the kingdom of heaven. And our souls long for it like we long for home. It is where you will be a thousand years from now and where we will spend eternity.

So how does this context shape or impact our lives? In the midst of a battle in which God is "showing himself to be holy," he encourages you and me not to get caught up in this seen world but to somehow stay focused on the unseen.

Since, then, you have been raised up with Christ (unseen), set your hearts (unseen) on things above (unseen), where Christ is seated at the right hand of God (unseen). Set your minds (unseen) on things above (unseen), not on earthly things (seen). (Col. 3:1-2)

This aspect of the context is so simple and so mundane that we usually fail to see just how profound it is. To put it bluntly, all that Jesus is inviting you to—life in the larger story—can only be found and experienced in the unseen realm. It is the only ticket. There is no other way.

And yet, I spend most of my day covered up by the business of my seen world. It's a trap that my flesh is addicted to. Try stopping and leaving this seen world to go be with Jesus in the unseen. Try practicing any type of Sabbath rhythm and see what happens. I work with people in ministry who refuse to take any type of sabbatical because their significance is tied to the seen world of what they do. The very nature of Sabbath was designed to make us stop and remind us that we don't make our worlds turn. The excuses we use for not stopping are rationalizations that are always cloaked and covered with seen-world trappings. Try taking a day away, a Sunday, to cease your seen world obligations and enter the unseen world to be with Jesus. A small war will take place between the seen and the unseen, between the enemy and God, who is jealous for our affections. How many folks do you know, in our present culture, who practice giving God one twenty-four-hour day each week? It's crazy. It is other-world thinking to do that. Let me bring it closer to home.

How hard is it to keep our fundamental priorities? Most of us would say, "God first, family second, work third, or church and then other things." Notice that the first two are relationship-focused. Why is it so hard to keep relationships a priority? It's because a key aspect of relationships is that they function mostly in the unseen realm. It's hard because the flesh is not drawn to the unseen. The unseen realm is mystical; it can't be controlled. And it's also hard because the enemy does not want us to go there. He does not want you to put the unseen over his seen dominion. When you and I try to keep these priorities, we're swimming upstream, against the current of our present culture and against the enemy who's behind it. If we try and wake up early in the morning each day to be with the most important facet of our lives, the God of the Universe, what will we find? I find a battle. It's a fundamental battle over what wins our affections, our first love.

Jesus invites us to the simple profoundness of the unseen realm. It is a huge part of the context we will need in order to discern all that God is doing in the larger story and what he is inviting us to. God is in the process of showing himself to be holy, and he chooses to pull you and me into the unseen realm to make that happen.

4
Faith

This is the last stone in the foundation of context. God is doing something to make his name holy (Chapter 1). He is doing it in the midst of a battle between good and evil, between himself and the enemy (Chapter 2). And this battle draws us into the unseen realm, the kingdom of heaven (Chapter 3). The last stone is the muscle that moves us up the pyramid. It is the idea or thought that allows us to function in the larger story. And it's the means by which we take hold of the life that Jesus invites us to. This stone is faith.

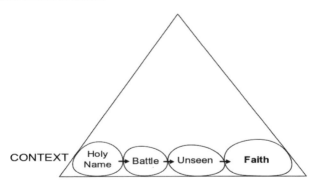

The writer of Hebrews describes it like this: "Now faith is being sure of what we hope for and certain of what we do not see" (Heb. 11:1). Did you catch the "do not see" part? Do you recognize how faith flows out of and is built upon the idea of the unseen? So it comes as no surprise, then, that if Jesus is inviting us to an unseen realm, faith will be the muscle that moves us into that realm. And it shouldn't surprise us that that muscle or action is what most pleases God.

> "And without faith it is impossible to please God, because anyone who comes to him must believe that he exists and that he rewards those who earnestly seek him" (Heb. 11:6).

As creatures, if we are looking for the one thing that will make our Creator smile, the one thing that warms his heart, we have found it. It is faith. And it has been that way from the beginning.

Did it surprise you that obedience is not higher on the list? Adherence out of the power of the flesh can lead to pride and independence. It was the hallmark of the Pharisees, and it is a stench in the nostrils of Jesus. Faith by its very nature is founded on humility and dependence and leads to an obedience that is empowered by a different source. Consider this: Would you rather have your child be obedient to you simply out of conformity to one of the ten commandments, to the law, or out of trust based on years of sacrificial love and faithfulness on your part? Ideally, you would want their response to emerge out of a relationship built on faith and trust. It is just like that with the Father.

We have been saved by faith—and faith alone—from the very start. "By faith Abel offered a better sacrifice than Cain did," and he was commended for it (Heb. 11:4). "By faith Noah, when warned about things not yet seen, in holy fear built an ark to save his family" (Heb. 11:7). Noah believed the words God spoke and built a contraption that he had probably never seen before nor had any concept of. He simply trusted God and that faith

40

led him to do what God told him to do. By faith, Abraham left his home and followed God to a place he had never been (Heb. 11:8-10). He looked at the stars and believed that his descendants would be numbered in the same way. He did this solely on the promise of God, even though he and Sarah were childless and barren at the time. And because of Abraham's faith, it was credited to him as righteousness (Gen. 15:6). He was made clean, righteous, because of his faith (Rom. 4:3). By faith, Isaac blessed Jacob over Esau (Heb. 11:20).

By faith, Moses followed the voice in a burning bush, confronted the most powerful man in the world, and led Israel to save its firstborn by slaughtering and spreading the blood of innocent lambs on their doorposts. By faith, the Red Sea parted. By faith, Joshua crossed the Jordan River and defeated Jericho. By faith, David defeated Goliath. By faith, Solomon built a temple. By faith, Elijah confronted the prophets of Baal. Notice that the basis of their salvation was not the feats they performed nor rewards for their obedience to the law. It was their faith in a person, and the promise made by that person, who moved them to action. Faith always precedes action and, ultimately, the act of following. It is always our belief that moves us and dictates how we live. Our actions reveal what we really believe. It's our lack of faith that condemns us, that paralyzes us, preventing us from following. Tozer writes,

> High up on the list of things which the Bible teaches will be the doctrine of faith. The place of weighty importance which the Bible gives to faith will be too plain for him to miss. He will very likely conclude: Faith is all-important in the life of the soul. Without faith it is impossible to please God. Faith will get me anything, take me anywhere in the Kingdom of God, but without

faith there can be no approach to God, no forgiveness, no deliverance, no salvation, no communion, no spiritual life at all. [1]

Andrew Murray says,

> Faith is the organ or sense for the perception and apprehension of the heavenly world and its blessings...Is it not the confession of nothingness and helplessness, the surrender and the waiting to let God work? Is it not in itself the most humbling thing there can be—the acceptance of our place as dependents, who can claim or get or do nothing but what grace bestows? Humility is simply the disposition which prepares the soul for living on trust. [2]

Tozer and Murray emphasize faith as the muscle that enables us to move in the unseen realm. For Tozer, faith gets us everything, and without it we have nothing. One of Murray's favorite themes is that of dependence. Faith is the model for what dependency looks like in a relationship with God. Faith is centered on God and his work instead of on us and what we can perform or do.

Back in Chapter 1, we noted that God is the one doing something. It is he who is showing himself holy. And it is he who is going to do it through you. If that's the case, then what should our response be to a God who is moving, acting, and doing it all? Faith is the definitive answer to what God is asking from us. God alone can show himself to be holy. God alone can make it happen. And God alone will get the credit. In the end there will be one parade, one celebration, for one person, because one person did it all. God didn't do most of it. He did it all. And our response is to trust him.

God includes us. He gives us a role. He works through us. Our response to him in this role is a dependent trust and faith in him. Ask Noah who built the boat. Ask Moses who parted the sea. Ask David who killed Goliath. God is showing himself holy, and we are putting our faith in his ability to pull it off. This dependent faith opens so many doors and windows. It opens our eyes, our perceptions, and our ability to comprehend the larger story. Context should help us see exactly what God is doing and the response he requires of us.

Jean-Pierre De Caussade writes,

> We live as we see and feel, and make no use of the light of faith which would guide us so safely though all the labyrinths, darkness and fantasies among which we wander foolishly for lack of faith which sees God, and only God, and lives always in him, leaving behind and going beyond appearances. Faith is the light of time, it alone recognizes truth without seeing it, touches what it cannot feel, looks upon this world as though it did not exist, sees what is not apparent. It is the key to celestial treasures, the key to the unfathomable mystery and knowledge of God. Faith conquers all the fantasy of falsehood; through faith God reveals and manifests himself, deifying all things. Faith removes the veil and uncovers eternal truth. When souls are given the understanding of faith, God speaks to them through all creation, and the universe becomes for them a living testimony which the finger of God continually traces before their eyes, the record of every passing moment, a sacred scripture.[3]

I hope it's evident that God is not looking for a performance from you and me. That is so much of what I grew up with. In all the years that I've done ministry, most of the people I have been around adhere to a paradigm of Christianity—of religion, in general—that has a strong sense of performance in it. If I could articulate the paradigm, it would sound something like this: Jesus came and lived a life that is the example for all of us to imitate. The emphasis seems more on sinning less, not living like Jesus. He died on the cross to remove my sins so that I can have a relationship with him and go to heaven. This relationship is now based on what I owe him: service, hard work, dying to myself, servanthood, all with an attitude of thankfulness.

And after all this reimbursement, there's still a feeling of insecurity; I'm haunted by the hope that my performance will be enough to win his acceptance, to get me in. This paradigm is full of great truths, but they are twisted just enough with the lie of self-sufficient performance that its true meaning has been lost. My fear is that what I've described is both familiar and comfortable to most of us. The question is, is this it? Is my performance all there is? Is this life beyond our wildest dreams?

Jesus is inviting you and me to a relationship based on dependent faith. It's a faith in him and in what he's promised. It's a faith that's about him and that he sits in the center of. It's a faith in the finished work of the cross he died on and in its ability to transform you and me. It's a faith based on facts—namely, the fact that he will see the task to the end, finished, completed. Jesus does it all. Lewis Sperry Chafer writes in *He That is Spiritual*,

> Christian character, therefore, is not developed, or "built" through human attention and energy...Human nature in its most favorable conditions has never been expected to do this...The fact, however, that He has designed that they shall be the "fruit of the Spirit" changes the whole human responsibility. It is no longer something for the human strength to attempt, nor is it to be done by the human strength plus the help of the Spirit. It is not something man can do, even with help. It is the "fruit of the Spirit." True Christian character is produced in the believer, but not by the believer. Doubtless the Spirit employs every faculty of the believer's being

to realize this priceless quality of life; yet there is nothing in the believer, of himself, which could produce this result. There is not even a spark of these graces within the human nature which might be fanned into a fire. All must be produced in the heart and life by the Spirit.[4]

Jesus, through his Spirit, is doing it all and is asking us to trust that fact. It's faith in a person and his promise. And the benefit is ours, by faith, if we believe it.

The Scriptures spend less time defining faith, and more time showing what it looks like in people's lives. In John 3, Jesus gives us the best analogy of what it means to trust and believe. A. W. Tozer describes it like this,

> In the New Testament this important bit of history is interpreted for us by no less an authority than our Lord Jesus Christ Himself. He is explaining to His hearers how they may be saved. He tells them that it is by believing. Then to make it clear He refers to this incident in the Book of Numbers. "As Moses lifted up the serpent in the wilderness, even so must the Son of man be lifted up: that whosoever believeth in him should not perish, but have eternal life" (John 3:14). Our plain man in reading this would make an important discovery. He would notice that "look" and "believe" were synonymous terms. "Looking" on the Old Testament serpent is identical with believing on the New Testament Christ. That is, the looking and the believing are the same thing. And he would understand that while Israel looked with their external eyes, believing is done with the heart. I think he would conclude that faith is the gaze of a soul upon a saving God.[5]

There are three observations about faith to point out from this analogy. First, faith is continuous. It's all day long, every minute of every day. It's not a glance; it's a gaze, a long hard continuous look. In the story above, the Israelites were instructed to look or gaze upon the serpent and they would be healed. I don't get the sense

45

that people would just walk by, take a peek, be healed and head home. There wasn't a waiting line. It wasn't like a vaccination. I get the impression that people were dying everywhere, and that as long as they set their gaze upon the serpent, they would continue to be healed or saved. If their attention strayed, they could be bitten. If they looked away, the healing stopped. It wouldn't take long to understand what was needed in this situation—a continual gaze. Likewise, Jesus is not inviting us to a one-time act of mental assent or belief when we enter into a relationship with him. He invites us to so much more—a life lived in continuous, dependent faith.

Jesus himself modeled this. As Tozer observes, "Indeed Jesus taught that He wrought His works by always keeping His inward eyes upon His Father. His power lay in His continuous look at God."[6] This life, this dependent life of faith, (which we'll explore more closely in the next several chapters) is a life that, I promise, will surprise us. It will not fit into our old paradigms, our old cisterns (Jer. 2:14) or wineskins (Matt. 9:17). Jesus wants to introduce us to something radically new. He did not come to deliver a new set of rules. He came to introduce us to a whole new way of living. Life beyond our imagination. A life that is all ours, by faith—if we will believe it, if we trust it.

The second aspect of faith is related to the first—it is like a gaze, but now our intense stare is on the object of what we are looking at. To believe in Jesus is to focus our concentration, our trust, on Him. The emphasis is on the object of our attention. Paul uses the phrase "set your minds on things above, not on earthly things" and "set your hearts on things above, where Christ is seated at the right hand of God" (Col. 3:1-2). The writer of Hebrews says, "Fix your eyes on Jesus, the author and perfecter of the faith" (Heb. 12:2). Faith is this constant setting of our attention or awareness on God, on the presence of God, like our life depends on it. The secret and the power is not in the intensity of our staring but in the object of our attention and trust. This will make so much more sense as we move forward in the next few chapters. It is a life focused on the most incredible person in the world. By faith, his presence will permeate our lives—if we believe it, if we trust it.

And third, faith brings no attention to itself. Tozer reminds us of this:

> Faith is the least self-regarding of the virtues. It is by its very nature scarcely conscious of its own existence. Like the eye which sees everything in front of it and never sees itself, faith is occupied with the Object upon which it rests and pays no attention to itself at all…Faith is a redirecting of our sight, a getting out of the focus of our own vision and getting God into focus…Faith looks out instead of in and the whole life falls into line.[7]

This thought fits with the concept that God is doing something and that the story is about him. Faith doesn't bring attention to us. It keeps the attention on Jesus, "the author and perfecter of the faith." This dependent, trusting faith gives credit where credit is due. God is the one doing the work, and ultimately, all the praise and glory will go to him.

Do you believe it? Do you really? Ezekiel heard all that God was about to do, that God was going to make his name holy, through you, before their eyes. Perhaps Ezekiel wondered if God could really pull this off. Well, in Chapter 37, God takes Ezekiel out to a valley of dry human bones. Interestingly, Paul evokes this picture when he writes, "you were dead in your transgressions and sins" (Eph. 2:1). So how dead were these bones? A little dead? Recently dead? They were as dead as dead can be. The concept of dead is connected to powerlessness or helplessness. These bones were powerless to do anything to save themselves. How helpless? They were as helpless as helpless can be. Then God told Ezekiel to prophesy to the bones. And the bones (which were powerless, having no ability within themselves) began to move and make a rattling noise. They grew together—bones, tendons, flesh, and skin. And God told Ezekiel to speak breath into them, and they became alive. Friend, these bones are you and me. We were once spiritually dead, helpless to save ourselves, objects of wrath. But the God of our dreams came and he spoke. And those bones, you and I, "came to life and stood up on their feet—a vast army" (Ezek. 37:10). God showed Ezekiel he could pull it off. And by faith, we became alive—if you believe it, if you trust it.

These first four chapters have been a foundation built with the stones of context. The next three chapters will be about the good news of the gospel of Jesus Christ. They will examine the cross and all that God accomplished there. Without context, it's possible we might misconstrue what God has done for us. But this is what we know for sure. There will be nothing at the cross that you can take hold of by force. There is nothing there that you can work for. The only way to appropriate any of the blessings of the cross is by a dependent trust. It's all yours, by faith, life beyond your imagination—if you believe it.

5
Forgiveness

When people talk about Jesus, they usually start with the cross. The most critical piece of the gospel, to be sure. But the cross can lose much of its meaning if it is not seen through the lens of context. As we've seen in the first four chapters, God is doing something for the sake of his Holy Name. He is doing it in the midst of a battle. Jesus comes and invites us to life in another, unseen realm. And we can only appropriate this life by faith.

This foundational context leads us back to Ezekiel in the Old Testament. If you remember from Chapter 1, Ezekiel 36:23 reveals to us the big picture. God is "showing himself holy, through you, before their eyes." So, what's the plan? In verses 25-27, God tells us how he's going to do it. And this is good news, not just for the Israelites in Babylonian captivity, but it's also the good news of the gospel of Jesus Christ for us, prophesied 550 years before his work on the cross. In verse 25, God says, "I will sprinkle clean water on you, and you will be clean; I will cleanse you from all your impurities and from all your idols." This is great news.

In the pyramid, I refer to this clean-water cleansing as Forgiveness. Illustrated on the second level of the pyramid, this will be the first of three aspects of God's redeeming work on our behalf. Jesus, by his work on the cross, is going to cleanse you and me of our sins. He is going to procure for us forgiveness. This is the Old Testament version of the gospel we are familiar with: Jesus dying on the cross for the sins of the people. But how did the death of one man accomplish this? How did Jesus' dying win forgiveness?

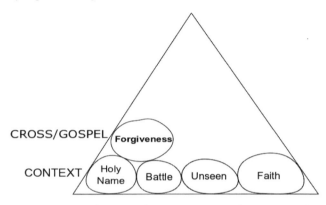

From the very beginning, God's method for dealing with our sin involved the shedding of blood. When Adam and Eve sinned, they were ashamed and covered themselves with fig leaves. But their response was inadequate. "The Lord God made garments of skin for Adam and his wife and clothed them" (Gen. 3:21). This was the first recorded shedding of blood. Later, Cain and Abel brought offerings to the Lord (Gen. 4:2-5). Abel's favorable offering from the flock was made possible by the shedding of blood.

When Moses led the people out of Egypt, the final plague was the death of the firstborn. A family or household's only escape or salvation was through the blood of a one-year-old lamb—the Passover lamb—which they were to spread on the door frames of their houses. God would see the lamb's blood and pass over them (Ex. 12).

After the Israelites escaped Egypt, God gave the law to Moses and the people. According to the law, when a person sinned, they were required to bring to the priest an offering, usually an animal. The priest would kill the animal, shedding its blood as an atonement, as payment for sin. "In fact, the law requires that nearly everything be cleansed with blood, and without the shedding of blood there is no forgiveness" (Heb. 9:22). Once a year, on the Day of Atonement, the high priest would make an offering for all the people, the entire nation. This blood was a payment that atoned for all their sins. It was sprinkled on the Mercy Seat, the atonement cover of the Ark of the Covenant, so that God could no longer see the people's iniquities.

When Jesus comes, his death fulfills and, in many ways, does away with this entire system of atonement through the shedding of blood. John the Baptist sees Jesus and pronounces, "Look, the Lamb of God who takes away the sin of the world" (John 1:29). In Hebrews, the writer says,

For Christ did not enter a man-made sanctuary that was only a copy of the true one; he entered heaven itself, now to appear for us in God's presence. Nor did he enter heaven to offer himself again and again, the way the high priest enters the Most Holy Place every year with blood that is not his own. Then Christ would have had to suffer many times since the creation of the world. But now he has appeared once for all at the end of the ages to do away with sin by the sacrifice of himself. Just as man is destined to die once, and after that to face judgement, so Christ was sacrificed once to take away the sins of many people; and he will appear a second time, not to bear sin, but to bring salvation to those who are waiting for him. (Heb. 9:24-28)

And by that will, we have been made holy through the sacrifice of the body of Jesus Christ once for all. Day after day every priest stands and performs his religious duties; again and again he offers the same sacrifices, which can never take away sins. But when this priest (Jesus) had offered for all time one sacrifice for sins, he sat down at the right hand of God. Since that time he waits for his enemies to be made his footstool, because by one sacrifice he has made perfect forever those who are being made holy. (Heb. 10:10-14)

Christ sheds his blood once and for all. He can do this because of the nature of his sacrifice. He was God, lived a sinless life, shed his own blood, and died a substitutionary death. His is a blood superior to that of bulls and goats. The blood of animals simply covered our sin like a blanket so that God didn't see our iniquity. But Jesus' blood removes our sins. His blood cleanses us.

Wash away all my iniquity and cleanse me from my sin...Cleanse me with hyssop, and I will be clean; wash me, and I will be whiter than snow. (Ps.51:2,7)

I will cleanse them from all the sin they have committed against me and will forgive all their sins of rebellion against me. (Jer. 33:8)

Let us draw near to God with a sincere heart in full assurance of faith, having our hearts sprinkled to cleanse us from a guilty conscience and having our bodies washed with pure water. (Heb. 10:22)

This is the avenue to forgiveness. It is the only route. Chafer remarks on this forgiveness:

Divine forgiveness is never an act of leniency. God can righteously forgive only when the full satisfaction of His holiness has been met. The root meaning of the word forgive in the scriptures, is remission. It represents the divine act of separating the sin from the sinner. Human forgiveness is merely a lifting of the penalty: divine forgiveness is exercised only when the penalty, according to the terms of His infinite righteousness, has first been executed on the sinner, or his Substitute...The forgiveness was possible with God, only when there had been a full atonement for sin. So in the New Testament, or after the sacrifice has been made at the cross for us, we are told that the blood of Christ has become the sufficient atonement for our sins...All divine forgiveness whether toward the unsaved or the saved, is now based on the shed blood of Christ. His blood answers the last demand of a holy God.[1]

This is the basis of our acceptance or forgiveness by God. It is a complete acceptance, an acceptance that we can't earn or win. It's a gift that is given and can only be received by faith. Miles Stanford writes in *The Green Letters*,

Every believer is accepted by the Father, in Christ. "Being justified by faith, we have peace with God through our Lord Jesus Christ" (Rom. 5:1). The peace is God's toward us, through His Beloved Son—upon this, our peace is to be based. God is able to be at peace with us through our Lord Jesus Christ, "Having made peace by the blood of the cross" (Col. 1:20). And we must never forget that His peace is founded solely on the work of the cross, totally apart from anything whatsoever in or from us... God's basis must be our basis for acceptance. There is none other. We are "accepted in the Beloved." Our Father is fully satisfied with His Beloved Son on our behalf...[2]

God's forgiveness, acceptance, and love for us is amazing. The reality of it is hard to comprehend or accept. Oftentimes, because it seems so familiar, because we have heard it so many times, God's grace loses some of its luster and some of its appeal. George McDonald writes, "for nothing is so deadening to the divine as a habitual dealing with the outsides of holy things."[3] Our biggest enemy is ourselves, and we settle way too quickly for something less than or smaller than what God has intended. Jesus is offering you and me a love and forgiveness that is beyond our wildest dreams. How can I communicate the extent of this "beyond" to you? It's a crazy challenge, but I want to try.

I don't know how well you know the story of Jesus and his death on the cross. I'll assume you're familiar with the basics—that Jesus was God in the flesh and that he came and died as a sacrifice for our sins. Now let me tell you about a God, a love, a Jesus who pursued you. He came when you weren't looking for him, when you didn't think you needed him and, honestly, when you didn't want him. But he came anyway. It's just who he is.

> You see, at just the right time, when we were still powerless, Christ died for the ungodly. Very rarely will anyone die for a righteous man, though for a good man someone might possibly dare to die. But God demonstrates his own love for us in this: While we were still sinners, Christ died for us. (Romans 5:6-8)

And then, after years of ministry, in the prime of his life, Jesus is killed. Right? No, that is not how it happened. Jesus wasn't killed; he voluntarily laid down his life for you and me. Consider this: If you knew you were going to die and had some sense of when, where, and how your death would take place, would this information change how you live? What you would do differently? Well, Jesus was aware of all these things, and yet he continued to walk toward them. Did you hear that? Jesus knowingly walked toward death. And he did it because God loves you. Jesus could have walked away at any point. The night he was arrested, for instance, he could have fought back. In fact, he tells his disciples, "Do you think I cannot call on my Father, and he will at once put at my disposal more than twelve legions of angels" (Mt. 26:53). But that call was never made. Jesus laid down his life for you and me. Later that night,

> The chief priests and the whole Sanhedrin were loing for false evidence against Jesus so that they could put him to death. But they didn't find any, though many false witnesses came forward. Finally two came forward and declared, "This fellow said, 'I am able to destroy the temple of God and rebuild it in three days.'" Then the high priest stood up and said to Jesus, "Are you not going to answer? What is this testimony that these men are bringing against you?" But Jesus remained silent. The high priest said to him, "I charge you under oath by the living God: Tell us if you are the Christ, the Son of God." "Yes, it is as you say," Jesus replied. "But I say to all of you: In the future you will see the Son of Man sitting at the right hand of the Mighty One and coming on the clouds of heaven." (Matt. 26:59-64)

He could have defended himself. Instead, he told them exactly what they wanted to hear. He told the truth. He laid down his life for you and me.

When the soldiers stripped him, beat him, and mocked him by putting a crown of thorns on his head, he could have spoken a word, flashed his sword and walked away, but he didn't. He laid down his life for you and me.

He was led out and taken to Golgotha, the place of the skull, the place where they crucified criminals. When they arrived, the soldiers had nails and were ready for the ordeal of trying to nail someone to a cross. He could have put up a fight. But he didn't. He literally laid himself down, for you and me.

After three hours, it got dark, strangely dark. All the sins of the world, yours and mine, all the darkness rested on this one man, Jesus. After three more hours, Jesus cried out, "My God, my God, why have you forsaken me?" This exact entreaty can be found in the first verse of Psalm 22, written nearly a thousand years before the death of Christ. Read it! Seriously, stop and read the whole thing right now. It's important…I'll wait…. For the first time, with the sin of the world resting on his shoulders, Jesus experienced the penalty for your sin and mine: separation. In some mysterious way, the triune relationship of the Father and the Son and the Holy Spirit took on the sin of the world. For a brief period of time, Jesus felt and experienced what you and I deserve. "But your iniquities have separated you from your God; your sins have hidden his face from you, so that he will not hear" (Isa. 59:2). He lays down his life, as a substitute, for you and me.

Again, I want to make one thing totally clear in this chapter: Jesus died but was not killed. It normally took about twenty-four hours for someone to die on a cross. But Jesus, after just six hours, says, "It is finished" (John 19:30). Finished—in those days it was a word that was sometimes used on receipts to mean "paid in full." Then he says, "'Father, into your hands I commit my spirit,' and he breathed his last" (Luke 23:46). He lays down his life for you and me. In John 10, Jesus says,

> The reason my Father loves me is that I lay down my life—only to take it up again. No one takes it from me, but I lay it down of my own accord. I have authority to lay it down and authority to take it up again. This command I received from my Father. (John 10:17-18)

Jesus, because of the great love that he and the Father and the Spirit have for us, laid down his life, for you and me. This is truly incomprehensible.

This love washes us, but in a way that is beyond our wildest dreams. It doesn't just cover our sins, like a blanket, so that God doesn't see them. It makes them disappear; "as far as the east is from the west, so far has he removed our transgressions from us" (Ps. 103:12). There's more, more than you can imagine. It's not just our past sins that he removes, but all of them—past, present, and future. The sins we are going to commit tomorrow are already erased. It's incomparable. Let me bring this home for us. If we rated ourselves on a scale of one to ten, with one being irreparably bad and ten being good and perfect, what number would you give yourself? Pick a number, any number. Here's the point. Only tens get to heaven. Let me say it again: Only tens get to heaven. A holy and perfect God can only be in relationship with beings that are holy and perfect (i.e., Jesus and the Holy Spirit). Heaven is a place totally absent of evil. It is a place that is perfect. I'm not sure what number you gave yourself, but I don't stand a chance. It is hopeless. Outside of a miracle, outside of a savior, I could never be considered perfect. Christ's death on the cross, and our dependent faith and trust in his work there, turns us into tens. It makes us holy and perfect in the eyes of the Father. I don't feel perfect, and I don't look perfect, but God sees me through the blood of Jesus. It makes us acceptable.

It makes us acceptable as ambassadors.

All this is from God, who reconciled us to himself through Christ and gave us the ministry of reconciliation: that God was reconciling the world to himself in Christ, not counting men's sins against them. And he has committed to us the message of reconciliation. We are therefore Christ's ambassadors, as though God were making his appeal through us. We implore you on Christ's behalf: Be reconciled to God. God made him who had no sin to be sin for us, so that in him we might become the righteousness of God. (2 Cor. 5:18-21)

Christ's blood makes us acceptable as adopted sons. "In love he predestined us to be adopted as his sons through Jesus Christ, in accordance with his pleasure and will" (Eph. 1:5). The use of "sons" is not just an example of exclusive gender language common in older texts. All women have been adopted, not as daughters, but as sons. Only sons had the rights to inheritance in that culture, and we now all have an equal inheritance in Christ.

Because those who are led by the Spirit of God are sons of God. For you did not receive a spirit that makes you a slave again to fear, but you received the Spirit of sonship. And by him we cry, Abba Father. The Spirit himself testifies with our spirit that we are God's children. Now if we are children, then we are heirs—heirs of God and co-heirs with Christ, if indeed we share in his sufferings in order that we may also share in his glory. (Rom. 8:14-17)

It's an acceptance beyond your wildest dreams. It's a forgiveness, a love, that is incomprehensible.

And I pray that you, being rooted and established
in love, may have power, together with all the saints,
to grasp how wide and long and high and deep is
the love of Christ, and to know this love that surpasses knowledge... (Eph. 3:17-19)

It truly surpasses our knowledge. It's beyond what we can
imagine.

I have the privilege of leading a Bible study at
Mission Waco's Manna House, a drug rehab program designed for the marginalized. Nowhere else am I around a
group of men who are more desperately hungry for Jesus,
and I am humbled by them. When I introduce myself, in
the tradition of an AA meeting, I usually say, "My name
is Ronnie Smith, and I am a recovering ass#*$+." (my
wife's suggested edit) It's my true addiction: my sin nature. No one knows my sin like I do, and I'm pretty sure
that I'm blind to most of it. When I think of the story
of the prodigal son's return, I'm overwhelmed. Not because the Father would take the son back. I get that. That
part is almost feasible. But Jesus loves me, forgives me,
in a way that is beyond my wildest dreams. Here is what
I can't comprehend. You see, I haven't just wandered off
like the prodigal once or twice or even three times. I've
gone whoring after other gods over and over and over
again. I've strayed in big ways and small, but it's wandering all the same. When the prodigal son returned home,
his father lavished him with a robe and a ring and sandals. Well, in my unseen house I have closets full of robes,
a chest of drawers full of rings, and an equal number of
sandals. Do you have any idea how much God loves me?
I'm his favorite. I know it's a theological impossibility. I
just can't grasp his forgiveness any other way.

If you feel you're able to comprehend anything

you've read in this chapter about his love and forgiveness, then multiply that by about a hundred thousand,
and maybe then, we'll be close to what is actually real and
true about God's love for us. He is the God of our dreams,
who is faithful and loves us with an enduring love. He accepts us and forgives us with a love that is simply beyond
us.

6
Freedom

I start this chapter with the pyramid introduced in Chapter 3. Remember: the pyramid is just a visual aid. It helps remind us of the larger story.

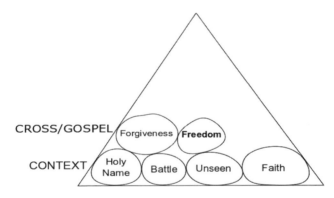

Again, the four sections on the bottom row of the pyramid represent context, which prepares us and helps us understand what comes next in the larger story. The three sections across the middle represent the cross or the gospel. The life that Jesus invites us to, a life beyond our wildest dreams, is represented in the upper half of the pyramid; it flows up and out of what Jesus has done for us on the cross. Forgiveness, acceptance, and love—discussed in Chapter 5—are the result of God's showing himself holy, in the midst of a battle, in the seen and unseen realms, and can only be gained by faith.

Did you notice that there are three sections to the gospel layer of the pyramid? And yet, in the previous chapter, we explored what most folks would consider to be the majority of the good news. In today's Christian culture, we have so emphasized the forgiveness aspect of the gospel that the thought of following Jesus, of being his disciple or anything else, has become a separate addendum. And it's an addendum rooted in the lie that, after all that God has done for us, it is finally our chance to do something, to give something back in return. We try and earn God's grace. But this is not the life Jesus is offering.

The life Jesus invites us into is connected to God's doing something through us. That life is found in and through the gospel. This section, Freedom, sits in the very center of that gospel. Incidentally, it also sits at the center of our pyramid. I wish I could say that I planned it that way, but I'm not that good. But it's appropriate that it's there. I think freedom in Christ is the best part of the gospel, the heart of the cross. Think of these three sections—forgiveness, freedom, and indwelling (which we'll look at in the next chapter)—as a meal, and all that you heard in Chapter 5 about Forgiveness was the appetizer. It's hard to imagine, isn't it? He's offering life beyond your wildest dreams. Are you ready for the main course?

> Come, all you who are thirsty, come to the waters; and you who have not money, come, buy and eat! Come, buy wine and milk without money and without cost. Why spend money on what is not bread, and your labor on what does not satisfy? Listen, listen to me, and eat what is good, and your soul will delight in the richest of fare. Give ear and come to

me; hear me, that your soul may live. (Isa. 55:1-3)

Ezekiel gives us handles for the gospel in an Old Testament context. In 36:23, he tells us God is going to show himself holy, through you, before their eyes. What follows is the plan for how he's going to do that. In verse 25, he declares that he is going to "cleanse you from all your impurities." We observed that forgiveness in Chapter 5. The second component of the plan, and the part that God uses to set us free, is found in the following verse: "I will give you a new heart and put a new spirit in you; I will remove from you your heart of stone and give you a heart of flesh" (Ezek. 36:26). God is going to take away our old heart and give us a new one. It's more than transformation; it's re-creation. Notice, he is not going to try and fix our old heart. He is going to do away with it. He is going to create a brand new one. This is the central plan of the cross. It represents freedom, and it is incredibly good news.

What shapes and molds this incredible plan is God's understanding of the totality of our problem. If we perceive the problem of our sin—all those transgressions we commit on a daily basis—merely as dirt, then all we need is a good washing. Better yet, if this is the only problem, then why don't we do the clean-up ourselves? Is this not the heart and soul of religion as the world knows it? Do not all of the world's religions have this at the core of their beliefs: the perception that people just need to overcome the dirt in their lives. Each religion has a plan to help them work out their own cleansing, their own efforts at self-improvement. Religion is focused on the dilemma of figuring out how to quit sinning. Christianity, when it has lost its way, pushes us toward this very thing. It pushes us toward trying to repair an old heart that even

God does not try to fix. Chafer says, "True spirituality does not consist in what one does not do, it is rather what one does. It is not suppression: it is expression. It is not holding in self: it is living out Christ."[1]

God has a solution for this problem, and it's radically different from religion. God alone knows the nature of the real problem, which is more than just dirt. It's a heart issue. You and I have inherited from Adam a sin nature, an old heart of stone, with roots from the rebellion still intact. This heart doesn't want God, will not choose God, and is selfish to the core. Jesus addresses this addiction to self and calls it slavery.

> Jesus said, "If you hold to my teaching, you are really my disciples. Then you will know the truth, and the truth will set you free." They answered him, "We are Abraham's descendants and have never been slaves of anyone. How can you say that we shall be set free?" Jesus replied, "I tell you the truth, everyone who sins is a slave to sin. Now a slave has no permanent place in the family, but a son belongs to it forever. So if the Son sets you free, you will be free indeed." (John 8:31-36)

We are all slaves to sin. We inherited it and have been slaves from the moment we were born. This life of slavery is all that we have known, and because of that, it has been hidden from us in the seen world. Like the Jews Jesus was speaking to, we are blind to its presence in our lives.

This next statement is simply born out of my own experience of slavery and has the authority commensurate with experience. My old heart seems wedded to the enemy, as though they have become one flesh. They seem to have a relationship, a connection, a direct form of communication. The enemy can whisper lies that speak right to the brokenness of my flesh and my old heart. It's like my old heart had been in captivity for so long that it had become, in some form, connected to what is evil. This is my experience of slavery. God's answer to this dilemma was a major transplant. The plan was not for us to fix or repair our corrupted old hearts. His answer was to create a new heart out of Christ's death and resurrection. Paul says it plainly to the church in Rome:

What shall we say, then? Shall we go on sinning so that grace may increase? By no means! We died to sin; how can we live in it any longer? Or don't you know that all of us who were baptized into Christ Jesus were baptized into his death? We were therefore buried with him through baptism into death in order that, just as Christ was raised from the dead through the glory of the Father, we too may live a new life. If we have been united with him like this in his death, we will certainly also be united with him in his resurrection. For we know that our old self was crucified with him so that the body of sin might be done away with, that we should no longer be slaves to sin—because anyone who has died has been freed from sin. Now if we died with Christ, we believe that we will also live with him. For we know that since Christ was raised from the dead, he cannot die again; death no longer has mastery over him. The death he died, he died to sin once for all; but the life he lives, he lives to God. In the same way, count yourselves dead to sin but alive to God in Christ Jesus. Therefore do not let sin reign in your mortal body so that you obey its evil desires. Do not offer the parts of your body to sin, as instruments of wickedness, but rather offer yourselves to

God, as those who have been brought from death to life; and offer the parts of your body to him as instruments of righteousness. (Rom. 6:1-13)

God's answer was not to fix our old heart but to kill it. How did he do that? He united himself with you and me. This is a move that only the God of your dreams can come up with. This union is laid out in Colossians as well. In Christ, we were circumcised (2:11), buried with him in baptism (2:12), made alive with Christ (2:13), died with Christ (2:20), and raised with Christ (3:1). He took us with him to the cross, and when he died, we died (Gal. 2:20). We have become united with Christ. We are "in Christ."

Christ's death was not only a substitute for ours, a payment of our debt. But he also died as a means for our freedom. Here's how others have articulated this union and the winning of our freedom.

> Andrew Murray: "Like Christ, the believer too has died to sin; he is one with Christ, in the likeness of His death (Romans 6:5). And as the knowledge that Christ died for sin as our atonement is indispensable to our justification; so the knowledge that Christ and we with Him in the likeness of His death, are dead to sin, is indispensable to our sanctification."[2]

> Watchmen Nee: "Our sins were dealt with by the blood, we ourselves are dealt with by the cross. The blood procures our pardon, the cross procures deliverance from what we are in Adam. The blood can wash away my sins, but it cannot wash away my old man: I need the cross to crucify me—the sinner."[3]

> Miles Stanford: "Our intelligent faith standing upon the facts of Calvary gives the Holy Spirit freedom to bring that finished work into our daily lives. We stood upon the fact of His dying for our sins, and this act of faith allowed the Holy Spirit to give us our freedom from

the penalty of sin—justification. Now, once we come to see the fact of the further aspect, we are urged in the Word to stand upon the liberating truth of our dying with Christ in His death unto sin, which allows the Holy Spirit to bring into our lives freedom from the power, the enslavement, of sin—progressive sanctification… As our Substitute He went to the cross alone, without us, to pay the penalty of our sins; as our Representative, He took us with Him to the cross, and there, in the sight of God, we all died together with Christ. We may be forgiven because He died in our stead; we may be delivered because we died with Him. God's way of deliverance for us, a race of hopeless incurables, is to put us away in the cross of His Son, and then to make a new beginning by re-creating us in union with Him, the Risen, Living One."[4]

Lewis Sperry Chafer: He has also entered into righteous judgements of our "old man"! And because of this He is now able to deliver His child from the power of sin. The "old man" is said to have been "crucified with him," and we are "dead with him," "buried with him" and are partaking in His resurrection life. All this, it is revealed, was to one great purpose, that "we also should walk in newness of life," even as Christ "was raised from the dead by the glory of the Father." What a deliverance and walk may be experienced since it is according to the power and glory of the resurrection! Resurrection, it may be added, is not the mere reversal of death; it is the introduction into the power and limitless boundaries of eternal life. In the new sphere and by the new power the Christian may now "walk."[5]

What a deliverance! All so that we may walk in a newness of life. It's an invitation to a radical new way of living.

Let me flesh this out for you in a familiar story from the gospels (Matt. 9:1-8; Mark 2:1-12; Luke 5:17-26). Jesus is teaching, and the crowd is overflowing the room, filling the doors and spilling out the windows. Aware of his healing powers, four guys desperately want to get their paralyzed friend before Jesus. So, they go to their friend's house, they pick him up on a mat, and they carry him out. When they come to the place where Jesus is teaching, they see the large crowd but are undaunted. They go to the roof, remove several tiles, and begin to lower their friend through a hole in the ceiling.

Have you ever wondered what this guy, the paralytic, was thinking? "What are you doing here? Where are you taking me? My hair! Look how I'm dressed! Jesus who? The healer? Is there a chance? I can't dare hope? Ah…look at the crowd, not here, please. Up there, there's no way. You guys are crazy! You're going to kill me! Go slow! What are all these people thinking? Jesus…so… this is you…you're the one?" Assuming that they lowered their friend in front of a standing Jesus, then his face is one of the first things the paralytic would've seen. I don't know what the face of Jesus looked like or what it was like to look in his eyes, but I bet from that point on, for the paralytic, it was all Jesus. He thought of nothing else.

Jesus said to him, "Friend, your sins are forgiven." I think the paralytic was the only person who really understood Jesus when he spoke these words. He was all too aware of his own sin, selfishness, and anger. Physical brokenness, after all, doesn't alleviate or excuse sin. Plus, when the words came, he was the only one Jesus was looking at. The Jewish leaders, meanwhile, upon hearing Jesus' words, asked, "Who is this fellow who speaks blasphemy? Who can forgive sins but God alone?" And as for the paralyzed man's four friends on the roof—even though their reaction was not recorded, I imagine them assuming that Jesus just needed a little help identifying the problem. I can hear them yelling, "Hey…It's the legs!" But this was the God of the paralytic's dreams. Jesus had not come just to offer him forgiveness but also to set him free. Jesus said, "I tell you, get up, take your mat and go home." The four men on the roof cheered, they laughed, they also put the tiles back in place on the roof, and then they celebrated with a friend who had been given the freedom of mobility. Jesus came to do more than wash away our sins.

Picture yourself in a desert, stuck on the side of the road with car trouble, no hope of rescue in sight. You finally see a car coming from a distance; it slows down, comes to a stop and lowers a window. It's Jesus. He smiles and says, "Friend, your sins are forgiven," then raises the window and drives off, leaving you sinless but still stranded. Is that the abundant life you've been dreaming of? Of course not. Christ didn't come to grant all your wishes and make you happy. He did come "to preach good news to the poor…to proclaim freedom for the prisoners and recovery of sight for the blind, to release the oppressed" (Luke 4:18). He has come to show the Father's name to be Holy, through you, before their eyes. He has entered a battle for you and has won your release. Some of the freedom you will experience is in this seen world, but most has been won for you in the unseen. And it's a freedom that will last forever. You will only experience this freedom by faith. And it's a freedom, a life that is beyond your wildest dreams. And Jesus offers this kind of freedom via a new heart.

Jesus wants to invite us to life beyond our imagination. This new heart we have been given is not a neutral heart. It's not new in the sense of "just out of the box" or "never been used." It is a noble heart, made from the DNA of Jesus. It has been formed out of the resurrection of Christ. It comes directly from him, and his new life gives you life. "We were therefore buried with him through baptism into death in order that, just as Christ was raised from the dead through the glory of the Father, we too may live a new life" (Rom. 6:4). Because of this new heart, we are now literally new creations, new beings. "Therefore, if anyone is in Christ, he is a new creation; the old has gone, the new has come" (2 Cor. 5:17).

If that's true, then this new heart also gives us a new identity. It's not only the beginning of our earthly transformation. It is the beginning of becoming what we should call "new creatures." When we die, our old heart and old body will stay right here on earth. Our old names will be on tombstones marking our death and burial. But our new heart won't be there. It will be with the new us, the new creature, in heaven. This new heart has always been the beginning of the new us. It marks us as brothers, sisters, and heirs with Jesus. It marks us as adopted children of the Most High God. When we get to heaven, we will be given new bodies to go with our new hearts. And we will be given new names to go with those new bodies, our new hearts, and our new identities. The new you, your new identity, is already here. You received it the moment you trusted Christ. Jesus is inviting you to reckon yourself dead to your old heart and to live out of your new heart, this new identity.

He's inviting you and me to become awakened to something new. Paul says, "I pray also that the eyes of your heart may be enlightened in order that you may know the hope to which he has called you, the riches of his glorious inheritance in the saints" (Eph. 1:18-19). I think that this hope, these glorious riches, are connected to our new identity. In Philippians 3:16, we are told to "live up to what we have already attained." It is both what

God has already given us and what he has called us to. I pray that God would enlighten the eyes of your new heart to a life and an identity beyond your wildest dreams. The new you!

7
Indwelling

On our pyramid, this is the last of the three sections that represent the work of the cross or the good news of the gospel. If the gospel is a three-course meal, then this is the dessert. In Ezekiel 36, God says he will show himself to be holy, through you, before their eyes. It is the theme of the plot of the larger story. As we saw in Chapters 5 and 6, he is going to do this through us by removing our sin and forgiving us. And he is going to do this through us by setting us free from the sin that had captured and enslaved us. He sets us free by killing our old heart and giving us a new and noble heart to live out of. He gives us a new identity. So here is the third piece. If your soul is starving for good news, welcome to dessert.

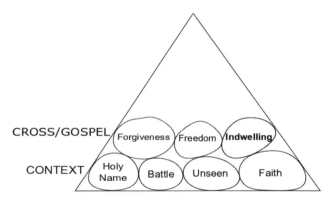

In Ezekiel 36:27, the Lord says, "And I will put my Spirit in you and move you to follow my decrees and be careful to keep my laws." God is going to put his Spirit inside of us. It makes sense. In order for God to do something through us, you would think that he would have to be in us in some form or fashion. But God could have chosen to do that by just visiting us. He could have anointed us with his Spirit like he did with the Old Testament kings and prophets. In that way, we would get the Spirit for a while, just when we needed it, when it was useful. Instead, he chose to indwell us. He chose not just to visit, not just to show up at Christmas and Easter, not just on Sundays, and not just for 30 minutes in the morning. He chose to live and make his home in us. He came to stay.

We read this and think, "Yes, I got that. It's just another piece of information about all the things you need to know about being a Christian." But stop! Hold the Presses! The God of the Universe has come to live inside you. That's right, inside you and me, the broken, dirty vessels that he has redeemed. The vessels he bought out of slavery, washed and set free. The Most High God lives inside of us. He goes where we go. God is everywhere, but now in some special way, he is in you and you bring him to the scene. Now God actually can, literally, do something through you.

In the New Testament, this thought is most clearly seen as Paul speaks of the body of Christ (Rom. 12:3-5, 1 Cor. 12; Eph. 4). This idea of the body is spoken in relation to the unity of our call and purpose. We are united in what God is doing as one body, in which Christ is the head. It is also spoken in relation to our unique giftedness and how God has individually designed us. It speaks to how he has empowered us to use that unique gifted-ness within the body. There are different gifts, different members, but one body.

However, this idea of Christ's body also carries with it the simple concept of a container. Wherever the body goes, Christ goes. Our bodies carry or take Jesus with us. Jesus is working, speaking, loving in us and through us. It is the heart of incarnational ministry. We get the privilege of seeing the Spirit flesh out Jesus through us. We get to watch, along with all the nations, the angels and demons, what God is doing in us. Robert E. Coleman writes in *The Master Plan of Evangelism*,

> By the same token it was only the Spirit of God that en-abled one to carry on the redemptive mission of evan-gelism. Jesus underscored this truth early in relation to His own work by declaring that what He did was in co-operation with "the Spirit of the Lord." It was by His vir-tue that He preached the Gospel to the poor, healed the brokenhearted, proclaimed deliverance to the captive, opened the eyes of the blind, cast out demons, and set at liberty those what were oppressed (Luke 4:18; Mat-thew 12:28). Jesus was God in revelation; but the Spirit was God in operation. He was the Agent of God actually effecting through men the eternal plan of salvation...In this light, evangelism was not interpreted as a human undertaking at all, but a divine project which had been going on from the beginning and would continue until God's purpose was fulfilled. It was altogether the Spirit's work. All the disciples were asked to do was to let the Spirit have complete charge of their lives. [1]

How does the Spirit inside us help? What role does the Spirit play? Again, there are books, entire volumes, writ-ten on the subject. So, whatever I say will not be exhaus-tive. But I will share with you the handles I hold on to that serve me and help me understand this indwelling.

There are three main things the Spirit does for believers. The first is seen again in Ezekiel 36:27: "And I will put my Spirit in you and move you to follow my decrees and be careful to keep my laws." The Spirit is going to "move us" to follow his decrees. The Spirit of God is the source of our enabling and empowerment. He is what literally "moves us." Without his power, we would not choose him. We clearly would not live outside of ourselves, sacrificially for others. And we would not choose to be like Jesus, follow him, nor share in his sufferings. The presence of the Spirit of God inside us is our empowerment for the entire Christian life.

Brother Lawrence humbly states in *The Practice of the Presence of God*, "Lord, I cannot do this unless Thou enablest me."[2]   Coleman says,

> They [the disciples] needed an experience of Christ so real that their lives would be filled with His Presence. Evangelism had to become a burning compulsion within them purifying their desires and guiding their thoughts. Nothing less than a personal baptism of the Holy Spirit would suffice. The superhuman work to which they were called demanded supernatural help—an enduement of power from on High. This meant that the disciples through confession of their deep-seated pride and enmity in utter surrender of themselves to Christ had to come by faith into a new and refining experience of the Spirit's infilling. The fact that these men were of the common lot of mankind was no hindrance at all. It only serves to remind us of the mighty power of the Spirit of God accomplishing His purpose in men fully yielded to His control. After all, the power is in the Spirit of Christ. It is not who we are, but Who He is that makes the difference.[3]

Chafer, following that line of thinking, writes,

> It is the Spirit of God doing something, and using the

believer to accomplish it; rather than the believer doing something, and calling on God for help in the task... Human energy, however, could never produce the divine results which are anticipated, and the Scriptures jealously contend that true Christian service is a direct "manifestation of the Spirit"...Spirituality is not gained by struggling: it is to be claimed. It is not imitation of a heavenly ideal: it is impartation of the divine power which alone can realize the ideal.[4]

These writers all agree that it is the Spirit that enables us to pray, serve, use our spiritual gifts, and more. Nothing in a spiritual sense happens outside of the Spirit. There is no life outside of the Spirit.

In my early years of ministry, I caught myself doing things for Jesus. When I look back on that time, I refer to it as the "Ronnie Show." I needed his help and his blessing to keep the show going. At times, it seemed more about me, my tasks and my ministry, than about him. I would speak of working for his name or his glory out of familiarity and good theology, but neither of them consistently motivated my heart. Most of this ministry was done through the power of the flesh, my abilities and talents. All of which are supernaturally powerless. God miraculously, in spite of me, used my efforts for the sake of his holy name. I grew to be hungry, though, for something else, something more, something that had power. The power that we read about in the Scriptures, in the New Testament.

I have been drawn to Paul's prayers for believers in Ephesus (Eph. 1, 3). I have already referred to some of these prayers in the previous chapter. But this time I want you to see how much Paul talks about power. For instance, notice that in Ephesians 1, he prays, first, that the eyes of their hearts would be enlightened to...

his incomparably great power for us who believe. That power is like the working of his mighty strength, which he exerted in Christ when he raised him from the dead and seated him at his right hand in the heavenly realms, far above all rule and authority, power and dominion, and every title that can be given, not only in the present age but also in the one to come. And God placed all things under his feet and appointed him to be head over everything for the church, which is his body, the fullness of him who fills everything in every way. (Eph. 1:19-23)

Did you notice how Paul went off about God's power? It is the power that raised Christ from the dead. It is the power that is going to restore everything to its rightful place. It is the same power that resides in you and me. It resides there because the Spirit, who is going to make all this happen, resides there. It is His power, the Spirit's power, that has become God's power in us. Paul is praying that you and I will come to comprehend that the mighty power of the Spirit is in us and working through us.

In Ephesians 3, Paul prays, "out of his glorious riches he may strengthen you with power through his Spirit in your inner being" (3:16; italics mine). He prays that you would be strengthened through his Spirit. That's what the Spirit does: He makes us strong. And he prays that the Spirit would make you strong in your inner being, in your soul, so that "Christ may dwell in your hearts through faith" (3:17). Paul prays that the Ephesians, "being rooted and established in love, may have power, together with all the saints, to grasp how wide and long and high and deep is the love of Christ, and to know this love that surpasses knowledge—that you may be filled to the measure of all the fullness of God" (Eph. 3:17-19). This power would enable us to believe, to grasp, to know just how huge, how gigantic, how completely humongous is the love of Christ for us. Paul prays that this power would allow us to experience the richness of having Christ reside in us. That this power would move us and enable us to comprehend his incomprehensible love toward us. It's a power beyond our wildest dreams. "Now to him who is able to do immeasurably more than all we ask or imagine, according to his power that is at work within us, to him be glory in the church and in Christ Jesus throughout all generations, for ever and ever! Amen" (Eph. 3:20). I'm telling you, he's inviting you to a life, a power, you can't imagine.

The second thing the Spirit does for believers is guide and lead them. One of the ways he does this is as a teacher. Jesus tells the disciples,

> I have much more to say to you, more than you can now bear. But when he, the Spirit of truth comes, he will guide you into all truth. He will not speak on his own; he will speak only what he hears, and he will tell you what is yet to come. He will bring glory to me by taking from what is mine and making it known to you. All that belongs to the Father is mine. That is why I said the Spirit will take from what is mine and make it known to you. (John 16:12-15)

In response to that passage, Chafer says,

> Here is a promise that the child of God may enter the highest realm of knowable truth as revealed in the Word of God. "All things that the Father hath" are included in the things of Christ and "things to come," and these form the boundless field into which the believer may be

led by the divine Teacher. This storehouse of divine reality will no doubt engage our mind and hearts for ever; but Christians may be even now entering and progressing in these realms of truth and grace.[5]

We have not received the spirit of the world but the Spirit who is from God, that we may understand what God has freely given us. (1 Cor. 2:12)

But you have an anointing from the Holy One, and all of you know the truth…the anointing you received from him remains in you, and you do not need anyone to teach you. But as his anointing teaches you about all things… (1 John 2:20, 27)

The Spirit of God guides us and leads us by teaching us. He brings to our remembrance truths in the Scriptures. "But the Counselor, the Holy Spirit, whom the Father will send in my name, will teach you all things and will remind you of everything I have said to you" (John 14:26). He uses the Word of God as a sword: "Take the helmet of salvation and the sword of the Spirit, which is the word of God" (Eph. 6:17). "For the word of God is living and active. Sharper than any double-edged sword, it penetrates even to dividing soul and spirit, joints and marrow; it judges the thoughts and attitudes of the heart" (Heb. 4:12). This guidance reveals to us the will of God. And it has an intellectual sense to it. We think of theology, ethics, right from wrong, truth and lies. The recorded word of God—the Bible, the Scriptures—will always be the most authoritative manner by which the Spirit of God reveals his heart, speaks truth to us, guides us, and leads us in these areas.

Another way the Spirit offers guidance is through the concept of being led or walking in the Spirit. Chafer writes,

In Romans 8:14 it is stated: "For as many as are led of the Spirit of God, they are the sons of God." This, it may be concluded, is the normal Christian experience according to the plan and purpose of God. It is equally true that some Christians are abnormal to the extent that they are not constantly led of the Spirit…The walk in the Spirit, or the life that is led of the Spirit, is one of the great new realities of this age of grace; yet some believers are so far removed from this blessing that their daily lives are shaped and adapted to the order and relationships of the past dispensation. It is one of the supreme glories of this age that the child of God and citizen of heaven may live a superhuman life, in harmony with his heavenly calling, by an unbroken walk in the Spirit. The leading of the Spirit is not experienced by all in whom the Spirit dwells; for such leading must depend on a willingness to go where He, in His infinite wisdom, would have us go.[6]

This idea of being led has both the essence of giving up control and also of following. These two concepts will be the focus of Chapters 8 and 9. For now, we'll stop and simply say that guidance is a major aspect of the Spirit's role in the life of the believer.

Have you noticed that each of these roles has a connection to the unseen realm? There is a power we can't see. There is a guidance that can't be seen or heard in any audible way, coming directly from the Spirit, who can't be seen.

The Spirit's third role is even more abstract. This last provision is related to his presence in us. From the very beginning, God has been a God of relationship. His very essence, the Trinity, is the source of all relationships. "The Word was with God, and the Word was God" before time started (John 1:1). God has been a God of covenants, of relationships. He has been a God in relationship through his presence in the Ark and in the Temple. And now, by indwelling us, he is doing the inconceivable. Angels were never referred to as "adopted sons of God," nor were they bestowed with all the rights and inheritance that come with adoption. Angels have never been referred to as "the bride of Christ." And yet Jesus has united himself to you and me. It is an intimacy that is unheard of, a mystery. And yet it is the very foundation of the life that Jesus is inviting us to. It is a life we could never have dreamed of on our own. And yet God has dreamed of it. He has a plan. He is going to make his name holy through us with this union. There is so much more to say, but not yet; it's coming.

This completes the second layer of the pyramid, the work of the cross. All three of these components of the gospel flow out of context. All three are part of God's plan to make his name holy, through you, before their eyes. All of these are an aggressive response on the part of God to do battle for you and me, to set us free. Jesus defeats death, sin, and the enemy at the cross. All these are unseen world realities. Our cleansing can't be seen. The heart that was taken and the heart that was given can't be found by a doctor. And the Spirit, by his very nature, can't be seen. His enabling power, his ability to lead, the intimacy that is closer than close—none of these can be seen by the naked eye. All three aspects of the gospel invite us to the unseen realm. And finally, all three segments of the finished work of the cross are appropriated by faith alone. We can't take them, earn them, or trade them. All three are gifts from God that we receive by faith, trust, and belief.

Everything above this second level of the pyramid and everything that we will talk about in the coming chapters will represent the life that Jesus invites us to. Would it be any surprise to you that this life flows out of the gospel of Jesus Christ and his work on the cross? Would it surprise you that this life is gospel-centered? The next two chapters rest on Jesus' finished work at the cross and resurrection. This good news has and will continue to define and empower the life he lays before us. And it's a life we could not have imagined. It is a life beyond your…well, you know what I mean.

8
Abandonment

For the next two chapters, we get to look at the life that Jesus invites us to. I have the daunting task of trying to do something that is way above my pay grade: describing to you a life that I believe is beyond what we can imagine, a life that's incomprehensible, a life beyond our wildest dreams. Lucky for me, it's a task that the Spirit of God loves to take on. It's his passion.

I love the emphasis at my church on being gospel-centered. It's based on the idea that the cross of Jesus sits in the center of all that the church is doing. It's a gospel that sits in the center of the larger story. I love this. It's fitting that in the pyramid illustration the Cross/Gospel level sits between Context and Life.

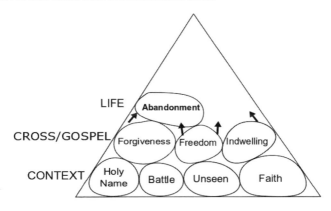

You would expect that whatever life Jesus is inviting us to—represented in the third level of the pyramid—proceeds out of the good news of the gospel. You would predict that the cross somehow dictates what the Christian life looks like. And it does. We are set free, redeemed out of slavery, by the death and resurrection of Jesus. Your old heart has been rendered dead, and you have been given a new heart. It's a payment, a ransom, an atonement made once and for all. The fruit of this is my redemption and my freedom.

I love the passages in Scripture that remind me of where I stand with God because of Christ's redemptive work on the cross.

> Do you not know that your body is a temple of the Holy Spirit, who is in you, whom you have received from God? You are not your own; you were bought at a price. Therefore honor God with your body. (1 Cor. 6:19-20)
>
> And they sang a new song: "You are worthy to take the scroll and to open its seals, because you were slain, and with your blood you purchased men for God from every tribe and language and people and nation. You have made them to be a kingdom and priests to serve our God, and they will reign on the earth. (Rev. 5:9, 10)

I have been bought, and my life is not my own. My soul has been purchased by the blood of the Lamb. I don't own myself; my life no longer belongs to me. It was true the moment I trusted Christ. It's true every day and all day long, and it tells me how I fit in the larger story.

There is another aspect to the Life that is every day, all day long and that flows out of the Cross/Gospel. What would you expect the Christian life to look like if you had two hearts—one that seems connected to the flesh and the enemy, the other to Christ? The first heart has been killed and rendered dead. The other heart, our new heart, comes from Jesus and his resurrection. Out of his new life comes our new life via a new heart. And it's ours by faith, not by obedience. What Christ has done to set us free, in giving us a new heart, can only be appropriated by believing. This faith, this continual gaze, invites us to something that looks like leaving one old heart and grasping a new one. It's a trust, born out of love, that produces obedience.

As a young Christian, I don't think I was ever told that I had two hearts. I was forgiven, a child of God, but I was still living out of my old heart. It was the only heart I knew how to live out of. When I tried to follow Jesus, I did it out of the energy of my old heart. I didn't know that there were any other options or possibilities. I don't remember Bible studies on this subject. There were no sermons, to my recollection. Who teaches these things to new believers? As I grew older, the authors I've been quoting from were the major voices I heard speaking to me on this subject.

This life that Jesus invites us to reflects the movement from the old heart to the new. This fits with what we know about the journey. Believers have been talking about dying to ourselves for ages. This transformation is a movement from death to life, from darkness to light. This life is about dying to our old heart and living out of our new heart. This is what the Scriptures attest to:

If anyone would come after me, he must deny himself and take up his cross daily and follow me.
(Matt. 16:24; Mark 8:34; Luke 9:23)
In the same way, count yourselves dead to sin but

alive to God in Christ Jesus. (Rom. 6:11)

You were taught, with regard to your former way of life, to put off your old self, which is being corrupted by its deceitful desires: to be made new in the attitude of your minds; and to put on the new self, created to be like God in true righteousness and holiness. (Eph. 4:22-24)

In Colossians 3, Paul chooses the verbs "put to death" (3:5) and "rid yourself" (3:8), followed by "clothe yourselves" (3:12) and "put on" (3:14). Notice that none of this just happens. We will not float there. We will not drift in to it. This transition takes an act of will. To pick up our cross daily, to deny ourselves, to follow him—all these actions drip with intentionality.

Each and every morning, we all wake up and put on clothes. Our clothes don't suddenly appear on our bodies. We have to choose what to wear and then put them on. The point is that when Paul says, "clothe yourselves" or "put on," he is saying, be intentional. He tells us to choose to believe. He summons us to count or reckon our old hearts dead. He's not telling us to kill our old hearts; that is something that Christ has already done. He's inviting us to appropriate truth. He's telling us to believe that what Jesus did for us is true. He's instructing us to put on our new hearts just like we put on clothes in the morning. Choose which shirt, choose which heart you are going to live out of today. The only difference is that you are going to have to put this new heart on over and over again, all day long, every day. It's what believers have been trying to do for the last two thousand years. It's a battle. And it's a battle we often lose.

If we are not intentional, guess which heart we'll find ourselves living out of. It's the heart that slides on most naturally. It's the one that's most comfortable, the old one we're familiar with. This is one of the reasons why this is such a struggle. We are learning how to do something new. We have never done it before, and it's radically different. It's neither familiar nor comfortable. How many times have you tried learning something new but gave up because it wasn't easy? G.K. Chesterton said, "The Christian ideal has not been tried and found wanting. It has been found difficult; and left untried."[1] If the Christian life you're living is not difficult and does not have a radically new aroma, stay hungry and keep looking. There is more.

I'm assuming this is not the first time you have heard this. The saints of old spoke about this as the anchor or pillar of the Christian life. When they talked about this putting off and putting on a new heart, they used words like abandonment, surrender, being yielded, and dying to self.

Andrew Murray writes,

> Jesus humbled Himself unto death, and opened the path in which we too must walk…His life, His person, His presence, bears the marks of death, of being a life begotten out of death…How can I die to self? The death to self is not your work, it is God's work. In Christ you are dead to sin…Place yourself before God in your utter helplessness; consent heartily to the fact of your impotence to slay or make yourself alive; sink down into your own nothingness, in the spirit of meek and patient and trustful surrender to God…The death to self has no surer death-mark than humility which makes itself of no reputation—which empties out itself and takes the form of a servant…What a hopeless task if we had to do the work! Nature never can overcome nature, not even with the help of grace. Self can never cast out self, even in the regenerate man. Praise God, the work has been done, and finished and perfected forever! The death of Jesus,

once and forever, is our death to self…Believer, claim in faith the death and the life of Jesus as yours…humble yourself and descend each day into that perfect, helpless dependence upon God…Sink every morning in deep, deep nothingness into the grave of Jesus; every day the life of Jesus will be manifest in you.[2]

Tozer writes,

The blessed ones who possess the Kingdom are they who have repudiated every external thing and have rooted from their hearts all sense of possessing. These are the "poor in spirit." They have reached an inward state paralleling the outward circumstances of the common beggar in the streets of Jerusalem; that is what the word "poor" as Christ used it actually means. These blessed poor are no longer slaves to the tyranny of things. They have broken the yoke of the oppressor; and this they have done not by fighting but by surrendering. Though free from all sense of possessing, they yet possess all things. "Theirs is the kingdom of heaven."[3]

Tozer goes on to talk about the story of Abraham and Isaac. He tells how Abraham loved Isaac to the point that his relationship with his son got between his relationship with God. God, being jealous for Abraham's affections, asked Abraham to offer Isaac, his only son, as a sacrifice to the Lord. This is a semblance of the passionate intimacy that God desires with each of us. It is a union so tight that there is no room for anything in between. We can resonate with the struggle that must've gone on in Abraham's heart. It is the same struggle that goes on in our hearts when we hear the voice of God compelling us to take the things we love most to the alter and offer them to him. The ache and pain of dying to ourselves, of putting God first and letting go of the cheap idols we cling to—idolatry—has never been bound by time. It's as real for us as it was for Abraham. Tozer writes,

> God let the suffering old man go through with it up to
> the point where He knew there would be not retreat,
> and then forbade him to lay a hand upon the boy. To the
> wondering patriarch he now says in effect, "It's all right,
> Abraham. I never intended that you should actually slay
> the lad. I only wanted to remove him from the temple of
> your heart that I might reign unchallenged there. I want-
> ed to correct the perversion that existed in your love.
> Now you may have the boy, sound and well. Take him
> and go back to your tent. Now I know that thou fearest
> God, seeing that thou hast not withheld thy son, thine
> only son, from me." …Now he was a man wholly sur-
> rendered, a man utterly obedient, a man who possessed
> nothing. He had concentrated his all in the person of
> his dear son, and God had taken it from him…Yet was
> not this poor man rich? Everything he had owned be-
> fore was his still to enjoy… There is the spiritual secret.
> There is the sweet theology of the heart which can be
> learned only in the school of renunciation…If we would
> indeed know God in growing intimacy we must go this
> way of renunciation. And if we are set upon the pur-
> suit of God He will sooner or later bring us to this test.
> Abraham's testing was, at the time, not known to him as
> such, yet if he had taken some course other than the one
> he did, the whole history of the Old Testament would
> have been different. God would have found His man, no
> doubt, but the loss to Abraham would have been tragic
> beyond the telling. So we will be brought one by one
> to the testing place, and we may never know when we
> are there. At that testing place there will be no dozen
> possible choices for us; just one and an alternative, but
> our whole future will be conditioned by the choice we
> make."[4]

This test is a regular occurrence in the believer's journey.
Jesus asks us to follow, and the very act of following means
we have to leave something behind. That something is
usually loved and cherished, even though it's sometimes
the very thing that's killing us. Sometimes what we have

to leave is our dreams. In order to follow the God who invites us to life, we might have to kill our dreams in order to be given new ones that are even better.

Jean-Pierre De Caussade, a spiritual director for the Visitation nuns of Nancy, France in the early 1800s, writes in *The Sacrament of the Present Moment*,

> For obedience to God's undefined will depends entirely on our passive surrender to it. We put nothing of ourselves into it apart from a general willingness that is prepared to do anything or nothing, like a tool that, though it has no power in itself, when in the hands of the craftsman, can be used by him for any purpose within the range of its capacity and design…they surrender themselves to God so as to have nothing but him, from him and through him. And so God becomes the source of life for these souls…That is to say that the sure and solid foundation of our spiritual life is to give ourselves to God and put ourselves entirely in his hands body and soul. To forget ourselves completely so that he becomes our whole joy and his pleasure and glory, his being, our only good. To think of ourselves as objects sold and delivered, for God to do with what he likes…A contrite and submissive heart opens the way to pleasing God. And ecstasy of perfect love pervades the fulfillment of his will by those who surrender to it; and this surrender practiced each moment embodies every kind of virtue and excellence. It is not for us to determine what manner of submission we owe to God, but only humbly to submit to and be ready to accept everything that comes to us.[5]

De Caussade invites us to a letting go and a dying to ourselves that is continual, all day long. It's an abandonment of control that finds God sovereignly orchestrating our circumstances. Though God doesn't cause evil, because he is in control, everything, good and bad, ultimately comes from his hand. In reference to this kind of abandonment, the saints used the phrase "living palms up," which means living in a state of receptivity. The opposite is striving—working constantly to maintain control in the midst of a battle. It's attempting to manage the craziness of our lives in a broken world. Jesus invites us to surrender, to let go and enter into a life we can't imagine.

Mary, the mother of Jesus, is an illustration of this. She is engaged to Joseph, and life couldn't be better. And then the Angel comes. He tells her she is going to have a baby, the Son of God. This is going to turn her world upside down. It could end her marriage. And what about her dreams? But listen to her palms up response: "'I am the Lord's servant,' Mary answered. 'May it be to me as you have said'" (Luke 1:38). Do you think this was the life Mary had imagined for herself? No, but it became a life beyond her wildest dreams.

What's it like to die to ourselves, to give up everything? What's it like to surrender our lives and become servants, slaves even, to someone else, to God? Is it worth it? De Caussade speaks to your new heart when he says,

> We long for the opportunity to die for God, and to live heroically. To lose all, to die forsaken, to sacrifice ourselves for others; such notions enchant us. But I, heavenly Father, will worship and glorify your purpose, finding in it all the joy of martyrdom, self sacrifice and duty to my neighbor. This is enough for me, and however your purpose may require me to live or die, I shall remain content. I love it for its own sake, apart from what it achieves, because it pervades, sanctifies and changes everything in me. Everything is glorified, all my moments are filled with your Holy Spirit, and, living and dying, I long only for it.[6]

Thomas Kelly writes in *Testament of Devotion*,

> The Cross as dogma is painless speculation; the Cross as

lived suffering is anguish and glory. Yet God, out of the pattern of His own heart, has planted the Cross along the road of holy obedience. And He enacts in the hearts of those He loves the miracle of willingness to welcome suffering and to know it for what it is—the final seal of His gracious love. I dare not urge you to your Cross. But He, more powerfully, speaks within you and me, to our truest selves, in our truest moments, and disquiets us with the world's needs. By inner persuasions He draws us to a few very definite tasks, our tasks, God's burdened heart particularizing His burdens in us. And He gives us the royal blindness of faith, and the seeing eye of the sensitized soul, and the grace of unflinching obedience. Then we see that nothing matters, and that everything matters, and that this my task matters for me and for my fellow men and for Eternity. And if we be utterly humble we may be given strength to be obedient even unto death, yea the death of the Cross.[7]

I want to live a heroic life. My new heart wants to live those kinds of lives De Caussade and Kelly talk about. Like Paul, I want "the fellowship of sharing in his sufferings, becoming like him in his death" (Phil. 3:10). The only way to life, to experience what God is inviting us to, is death. It's the path Abraham took when he offered Isaac. It's the path Mary accepted palms up. It's the ancient path that the prophets of old chose.

> This is what the Lord says: "Stand at the crossroads and look; ask for the ancient paths, ask where the good way is, and walk in it, and you will find rest for your souls." (Jer. 6:16)

It's the same pathway that Jesus took.

> Who, being in very nature God, did not consider equality with God something to be grasped, but made himself nothing, taking the very nature of a servant, being made in human likeness. And being found in appearance as man, he humbled himself

and became obedient to death—even death on a cross! (Phil. 2:6-8)

It's also the route Paul picked.

But whatever was to my profit I now consider loss for the sake of Christ. What is more, I consider everything a loss compared to the surpassing greatness of knowing Christ Jesus my Lord, for whose sake I have lost all things. I consider them rubbish, that I may gain Christ. (Phil. 3:7-8)

And it's the road Jesus is inviting us to.

Anyone who loves his father or mother more than me is not worthy of me; anyone who loves his son or daughter more than me is not worthy of me; and anyone who does not take his cross and follow me is not worthy of me. Whoever finds his life will lose it, and whoever loses his life for my sake will find it. (Matt. 10:37-39)

It's also the road my Young Life leader took. His choice to take this path and die to himself is why my life changed during my senior year of high school. I had trusted Christ several years earlier, but I had no sense of what a relationship with Jesus meant. My sister went to Young Life, but I hated it. All the folks I got drunk with on weekends went there, and all I saw was one ugly, hypocritical youth group. That senior year, I met Stan Eastin. Stan had a baby blue "Hippie" van with shag carpet. He had a Jesus beard and wore those big clunky leather hiking boots with his Wrangler jeans rolled up. He was so cool. I found out later that he had picked three guys to pray for every day, and I was one of those three guys. I first attended a Bible study called Campaigners, where I learned that Young Life was designed for me and all the kids I partied with.

A few weeks later I went to a Monday night "Club" meeting. I remember sitting on the floor with 150 other kids. Now, an important detail to note is that Stan was an introvert. That's what I liked about him. He was asked to lead the first couple of songs that night. They were fast songs, upbeat and unfashionably nerdy. Well, Stan was upfront, smiling, clapping, and singing. He was also sweating, even though it wasn't hot. His eyes said everything. He was nervous, out of his comfort zone, and hating it. Whether he consciously knew it or chose it, he was dying, dying to himself. I can't explain how or what happened next, but something in my head asked the question, "Why is he doing this? Why is he doing what he clearly doesn't want to be doing?" No audible voice answered, but the whispered thought came back, "He's doing it for you." ... From that point on, Stan Eastin had me. And Jesus had me as well. My life has never been the same. I smelled the death of Jesus that night. It was the fragrance of life, and it was all over Stan. I've been drawn to the aroma of death, the smell of Jesus, ever since.

There is only one path. It's the path Jesus took. And all the saints who have ever followed. And in the words of Tozer, "There will be no dozen possible choices for us, just one and an alternative, but our whole future will be conditioned by the choice we make."

9
Following

The third level of our pyramid has two sections, which together represent the Life Jesus invites us to. The eighth section, which we covered in the previous chapter, is titled Abandonment. Dying to self is what abandonment feels like from our perspective; submission or surrender is what it feels like when we're facing God. The word abandonment also carries with it the idea of moving from old to new. As we'll see, the next section, as with most of the pyramid, moves out of one section and into the other, from left to right. The first leads into and enables the second. So, death comes before life. Christ's life models this progression.

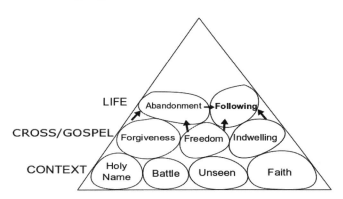

The Life Jesus offers flows up and out of death, his death

on the Cross/Gospel. It rises up from the second layer of the pyramid and into the third. This Life, the third level, is gospel-centered. It is life lived out of a new heart, empowered by the Spirit. If we are going to push this idea forward, we have to ask this next question. Since God has indwelled us with his Spirit—to empower, guide, and be intimate with us (all that we observed in Chapter 7)— what would you think this life looks like? Whatever the plan is, we know from context that God, the Spirit, will be empowering us in the midst of a battle that we can't see, and this guidance will require an intimate faith and trust. I'm convinced it is a life infused with the gospel and understood through context.

When Jesus calls his disciples, he has a standard invitation. Jesus says to Simon and Andrew, "Come, follow me, and I will make you fishers of men" (Matt. 4:19). His call to Matthew is similar: "Jesus went out and saw a tax collector by the name of Levi (Matthew) sitting at his booth. 'Follow me,' Jesus said to him, and Levi got up, left everything and followed him" (Luke 5:27-28). Follow me was the standard invitation or call to be a disciple, or follower, of Jesus. They left everything—their jobs, their homes, their families. Before they could follow, there was some sense of abandonment. They had to lose their lives. That's why I've placed Chapter 8 before Chapter 9. Commitment/abandonment always precedes intimacy/following. That's a rule in every area of life.

So, what does it mean to follow? In the Scriptures the word is used in two ways. One: A follower is someone who adheres to the teaching of a rabbi or Master. In the Old Testament, you were a follower of God if you kept the law, if you kept the Sabbath, if you adhered to the teachings of God. This is the smaller aspect of the word.

It represents the faith of the Pharisees, and yet sadly, it is still the standard of how most people today understand the concept of following.

The larger aspect comes from the concept of being led. God leads Abraham out of his homeland to a new land. He leads Joseph into Egypt. He leads Moses to confront Pharaoh. He leads the nation Israel through the Red Sea. He leads them with a pillar (Ex. 13:21-22).

By day the Lord went ahead of them in a pillar of cloud to guide them on their way and by night in a pillar of fire to give them light, so that they could travel by day or night. Neither the pillar of cloud by day nor the pillar of fire by night left its place in front of the people.

Notice: empowerment, intimacy, and guidance.

He leads Joshua into the promise land. Let's stop and take a look at how God leads Joshua. For forty years, while wandering in the wilderness, Joshua has been preparing to take and inhabit the promised land. When he and the people of Israel arrive at the Jordan River, Joshua is working on a plan for crossing. But God delivers his own. God, along with the Ark, goes before the people and, just like when they crossed the Red Sea with Moses, water walls up, and they cross on dry land. I'm sure this all went just as Joshua had planned. No! It was beyond his wildest dreams. When they get to the other side, God has Joshua completely incapacitate his entire fighting army. While in enemy territory, vulnerable to attack, with no path of retreat, all the fighting men are to be circumcised. This also, I'm sure, was part of Joshua's great military strategy from the outset. No way! God, on the other hand, is not worried about being defenseless in enemy territory; he is thinking about hearts. He's building faith.

When they get to Jericho, you have to think that Joshua is biting at the bit. He can't wait to use all his military training. He can't wait to show himself to be an excellent leader in front of all the people of Israel. He can't wait to execute the plans he's formulated and has been wanting to use for years. But God sends an angel. The angel tells Joshua to march around the city and blow horns for seven days. Imagine what Joshua must've been thinking: "You have got to be kidding. This is humiliating. No one conquers a city like this. What will people think? The other nations? Do I trust God or my own plan and abilities?" Well, you know the rest of the story: "And the walls came a-tumbling down." God is leading Joshua and, in doing so, is building Joshua's faith in him and him alone. And God's name is being made holy, through Joshua, before all their eyes: the eyes of Joshua himself, the eyes of the nation Israel, the eyes of all the nations surrounding Jericho, and even the eyes of angels and demons. There is intimacy, there is power, and there is guidance.

The prophets were men led by God. They, too, experienced intimacy, power, and guidance. From the beginning, God has been in the business of leading. Chafer writes,

> To be yielded to Him is to allow Him to design and execute the position and effectiveness of our life. He alone can do this. Of all the numberless paths in which we might walk, He alone knows which is best. He alone has power to place our feet in that path and to keep them there, and He alone has love for us that will never cease to prompt Him to do for us all that is in His wisdom, power and love to do. Truly the life is thrice blessed that learns to yield to the will of God. Nothing could be more misdirected than a self-directed life. In our creation God has purposely omitted any faculty, or power, for self-di-

rection. "O Lord, I know that the way of man is not in himself: it is not in man that walketh to direct his steps" (Jeremiah 10:23). It is the divine plan that the element of guidance shall be supplied in us by God Himself. One of the results of the Adamic fall is the independence of the human will toward God; yet man is most spiritual and most conformed to the design of his Maker when he is most yielded to the divine will.[1]

There is nothing inside us that was designed to direct ourselves. We have always been made to be dependent, to be led. Direction and leading were invariably God's to provide. Our old hearts want to usurp what belongs to God, and that is why those who walk in the flesh are considered lost and without direction. De Caussade describes it like this:

When one is led by a guide who takes one through unknown country by night, across ground without any clearly defined paths, going wherever he fancies without asking advice or disclosing his intentions, what is there but to surrender to him? What is the use of looking to see where one is, asking passersby, or consulting the map and other travelers? All this would defeat the intention and whim, so to speak, of our guide, who demands complete confidence and wishes to arouse anxiety and mistrust in us in order that we should totally depend on him. If we were certain that he was guiding us in the right direction, this would be neither faith nor surrender...Jesus Christ was the first born, without example or doctrine, always freshly inspired, his sacred soul obedient to every breath of the Holy Spirit. The Apostles lived more by the impact of his Spirit than by the imitation of his deeds. He never needed to look to the past for a precedent, he was moved by grace according to the pattern of eternal truths contained in the infinite wisdom of the Holy Trinity; and the orders he received moment by moment he outwardly obeyed. The Gospel shows us how these truths affected his life, and the same Jesus lives among us still, working ever freshly in saintly souls.[2]

Being led is clearly the larger part of following. It's powerful, dynamic. It's relational. It requires more faith, which pleases God. So, when Jesus asked the disciples to follow him, and they left everything, which way do you think they interpreted this word? Do you think they perceived it as adhering to or being led? Some thirty years later, when Peter is hanging upside down on a cross in Rome, dying a martyr's death, how do you think he heard it? How do you hear it?

When I lead spiritual retreats, I walk folks through a little exercise. I hope I can explain it well here. I usually ask one person (for the sake of this illustration, we'll call him John) if they think they can follow me around the room. The answer is always a befuddled "yes." Of course they can. In the same way, when the disciples were with a walking, breathing Jesus, they could literally follow him in the seen world. But after Jesus dies, is resurrected, and goes to heaven in the unseen realm, what does it mean to follow him then? To make my exercise mirror the Christian experience as closely as possible and because we can't see Jesus, I put a blindfold over John's eyes. And because I've never heard the audible voice of God, I tell John that I won't speak to him, nor will I touch or pull on him in any physical sense as I try to lead him. Jesus says to us, "Follow me," but we can't see him, feel him, or hear him. Do you think John can follow me now? My point is, how do we follow someone or something we can't see, hear, or touch in the seen world? It's almost impossible… in the seen world.

Keep following me if you will. What if I wrote John a letter (the Scriptures) and showed him my heart and where I'm going. What if he interpreted that letter as a map (the law), as directions (rules). This is what some of us have done with the Bible. The problem with this approach is that the map now gives John the option of leaving me and going on ahead and meeting me somewhere. The letter, the map has become the center of the relationship, and it gives John the option of being in control. This is the option of being a follower who adheres to, versus a follower who is being led. This is the option the nation Israel chose at the base of Mt. Sinai as they came out of Egypt. Instead of continuing to ride on the crazy wings of God's grace and being led by him, Israel's arrogant response was, "Tell us what to do and we will do it." And God gave them the law. The Scriptures were designed to be a reflection of God's heart that would draw us to him, not a map or set of rules that we could never keep and that the enemy would use to draw us away. The map is not the option that Jesus came to offer. He did not come to this earth to deliver a new set of rules. It's an option we have created that appears easier and appeases the flesh. Which would you pick: adhering to or being led? Your old heart would pick adhering to, and your new heart being led. And now you know why you feel that tension.

Staying with the analogy, what if I (Jesus) chose to do something new, something radical, beyond anything you can imagine? What if I chose to indwell you, to come live inside you? What would it mean to follow me now? If my spirit was inside you, empowering and guiding you, do you think you could follow me? You could, but it would be a completely different and an altogether new experience. The life God invites us to flows up and out of the Gospel, and *Indwelling* changes everything. It's one of the foundations of life beyond your wildest dreams.

Let's keep asking the question: What does it mean for us to follow? There is an old thought that I grabbed out of George MacDonald's The Curate's Awakening. The curate is struggling with the possibility that he has never done anything in response to the leading of the Spirit. "I thought to myself, 'Have I today done a single thing he has said to me? When was the last time I did something I heard from him? Did I ever in all my life do one thing because he said to me, "Do this?"' 'And the answer was, no, never.'"[3]

There is an underlying assumption in this passage that God communicates with us. What comes out of this is what I have termed "the basic question for the Christian life": **What have you heard Jesus tell you to do today, and have you done it?** This question is built upon the two major functions in following: awareness and response. This takes following out of the abstract clouds of intellectual thought and brings it into the practical world of reality. What have you heard Jesus tell you to do today, and have you done it? That's a question that invites me to be led.

Growing up in the Bible Belt, I had mastered working on the response component well before I ever knew the awareness component existed. Back then, my understanding of response was obedience. My understanding of awareness was skewed because I thought God had already spoken via the Scriptures and so he no longer speaks. I thought, if he can't communicate, then he can't lead. Awareness, therefore, was knowing the Scriptures. In my mind, awareness and response, following, simply meant being biblical. I had traded listening to and being led by a person for reading and studying a text. I have so much appreciation for the foundation that biblical knowledge has given me. I just wish I could have held it differently. I needed balance. And I needed someone to model it for me. Speaking solely from my own experience, that trade robbed me of power, guidance, and intimacy, and at times my life was more connected to adhering to than to following or being led.

Books have been written on awareness. Their titles contain words like contemplative, listening, and looking. They instruct us on a life with Jesus and the Spirit. They describe an attentiveness to the Lord and his leading. (I'm not going to expound on this now because it will be fleshed out in the next chapter, and I want you to discover it.)

The Scriptures invite us to an attentiveness:

> Since, then, you have been raised with Christ, set your hearts on things above, where Christ is seated at the right hand of God. Set your minds on things above, not on earthly things. For you died, and your life is now hidden with Christ in God. (Col. 3:1-3)

The Scriptures invite us to look:

> Let us fix our eyes on Jesus, the author and perfecter of our faith, who for the joy set before him endured the cross, scorning its shame, and sat down at the right hand of the throne of God. (Heb. 12:2)

The Scriptures invite us to listen:

> The man who enters by the gate is the shepherd of his sheep. The watchman opens the gate for him, and the sheep listen to his voice. He calls his own sheep by name and leads them out....I have other sheep that are not of this sheep pen. I must bring them also. They too will listen to my voice, and there shall be one flock and one shepherd...My sheep listen to my voice; I know them, and they follow me. (John 10:2-4, 16, 27)

The Scriptures implore us to stand firm and alert. This idea is repeated in Ephesians 6. Listen to the verbs and the actions in this chapter: be strong (6:10), put on (6:11), take your stand (6:11), put on (6:13), stand your ground (6:13), to stand (6:13), stand firm then (6:14), with readiness (6:15), take up (6:16), take (6:17), and pray (6:18), on all occasions (6:18), all kinds of prayers (6:18), be alert (6:18), always keep on praying (6:18). This is a biblical picture of the constant, continual attentiveness that Jesus invites us to.

Tozer paints a picture, using the words "spiritual receptivity":

> Why do some persons 'find' God in a way that others do not? Why does God manifest His Presence to some and let multitudes of others struggle along in the half-light of imperfect Christian experience?...I venture to suggest that the one vital quality which they had in common was spiritual receptivity. Something in them was open to heaven, something which urged them Godward...They had spiritual awareness and that they went on to cultivate it until it became the biggest thing in their lives. They differed from the average person in that when they felt the inward longing they did something about it. They acquired the lifelong habit of spiritual response...Let any man turn to God in earnest, let him begin to exercise himself unto godliness, let him seek to develop his powers of spiritual receptivity by trust and obedience and humility, and the results will exceed anything he may have hoped in his leaner and weaker days.[4]

What does this attentiveness look like in the real world, day in and day out? Let me share some of what it means for me. Some people say, "A man's heart is most alive when he is hunting." There are parts of our souls that are awakened when we sit or walk in silence, looking and listening intently. These are the same muscles we use in the unseen realm to hunt or look for Jesus. One day, I was waiting to get my oil changed when I picked up a hunting magazine. There was a story about Jim Corbett, the world's greatest tiger hunter, and his experiences in India in the early 1900s. I promptly went out and bought several of his books, wanting to steal whatever skills of attentiveness and observation this man had. I wanted to hunt Jesus with the same intensity as hunting for tigers. Put your camo on, and tell me how many times you saw Jesus today. What drills are you practicing this week to make you better at being with Jesus? Real life questions for a real life of being led.

The other thought I'd share is this. One of the things you pick up as an athlete is the idea of a "ready position." It is a concept that is ingrained in every player from the beginning. And it is true for all sports. You have probably heard it described as "feet shoulder-width apart, knees bent, weight on the balls of your feet, eyes up, hands ready." This position is standard for any player in any sport. It's an attentive position. It prepares the athlete for awareness and response. What does this ready position look like in the spiritual life?

Feet shoulder-width apart represents a good foundation. It's a foundation that comes from being grounded in the truth of his presence. Knees bent shows the readiness to respond. You're connected, praying, in communication, abiding. On the balls of your feet means you are not sitting back, you're trying to be intentional. Eyes up is having your head in the game. It's anticipating what's going to happen next. It's looking for your reads, clues, signals, all of which God is showing. Hands ready means you are prepared to do something: catch, throw, shoot, block, tackle, kick. Awareness and Response. Have you put yourself in a position, mentally and physically, to do what Christ is telling you to do? The hard part, toward the end of a game, is keeping this position. Fatigue causes us to lose this stance. We maintain this position by creating endurance through long, hard practice, balanced with taking sabbaths and staying rested.

I'll close with an illustration I use to help me grasp attentiveness and what I want to move towards in my experience of Jesus. Think of a pyramid. (Yes, another pyramid.)

The base constitutes the biggest area and represents most of my experience. Most days I get so caught up in the seen world that I'm oblivious to the constant presence of Christ. When I'm not intentional with his presence and his personhood, obliviousness is where I drift to every time. Other days, I'll see Jesus in hindsight. "Oh, that was you back there, Jesus. I recognize your presence now." It's an experience of Jesus in the past, but not in the present moment. It's like looking back and being thankful. That's the second layer, and it's often my experience. The third occurs even more seldomly. These are the times when it feels like Jesus is right there beside me. We are together. I'm usually doing something, needing him and feeling his presence with me. This is a great experience and one I'd like to keep all day long. But I'm also tempted to think this is as far as it goes and, therefore, might settle for something less. The top of the pyramid is the goal. It's what we long for. It is those brief moments when we are scared to death, hanging on, and Jesus seems to be flying in front of us. We are caught up in the wake of his leading. We are totally out of control, hanging on for dear life, and he's doing all the work. When the adrenaline rush is over, we catch ourselves saying, "That was the best week of my life." We would be hesitant to ever choose it again because our old hearts cling to control. But it is what our new hearts and our souls long for. It's what they're made for. It's a life of following, of being led, and it's beyond your wildest dreams.

10
Jesus

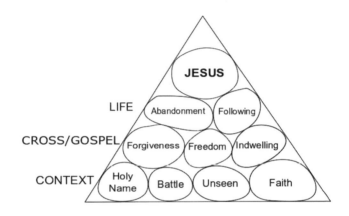

We have reached the top of the pyramid. This is it, life beyond your wildest dreams. Everything is right here, the epiphany, the crescendo. You would think that, if God is inviting us to life, there would be someone who has lived it in front of us, someone who has modeled it for us. Could it be Moses or one of the Prophets? How about King David, a man after God's own heart? One of the disciples, perhaps: Peter, James, John? Maybe even Paul? Jesus answers, "I am the way and the truth and the life. No one comes to the Father except through me" (John 14:6). Jesus claims to be the life. Surely, he of all people has lived it. And he has, just not in the way that you and I think about it. Jesus has lived the life and has invited the disciples and all of us to follow him. He's invited us to live the same life he did. That's what I've heard most of my life; I just didn't understand it. There's always been one problem: me. The problem is my old heart. There is no way I can live the life Jesus lived.

Most scholars think the synoptic gospels—Matthew, Mark, and Luke—were written early in the history of the Church, between 55 and 65 AD. They give us the life and teachings of Jesus from eyewitness accounts. They tell us many of the things he did, and there's an assumption, that we're somehow supposed to emulate this incredible life. But have you raised anybody from the dead lately? Have you cast out any demons in the last week? Neither have I. So, when I read the synoptics and hear the invitation to come live the life of Jesus, to be like him, there is a HUGE disconnect. Jesus was God, and I am not. He cheated. It seems he's asking me to do something that he was able to accomplish but that no other human could possibly do. Faced with this dilemma, we either have to do what Christian culture has done, which is to lower the bar, or we have to think differently. Can I introduce you to a new paradigm?

John was the last living disciple. He wrote his gospel account around the time of 85-95 AD. And as the last writer, he got to ask, "What is missing from the story; what have we not included?" In the book of John, he tells us something new. He tells us how Jesus pulled it off. He tells us how he performed the miracles. He shows us how Jesus lived the life. I'm going to try and give you two things at once. One is an accurate description of the life that Jesus invites us to, the life he lived, life that is beyond our imagination. The second is a biblical theology, from the book of John, of following or being led.

This biblical theology helps explain the emptying or setting aside of Jesus' divinity described in Philippians

2. How did Christ, being fully God, take on human flesh? This is a great mystery.

> Who [Jesus], being in very nature God, did not consider equality with God something to be grasped, but made himself nothing, taking the very nature of a servant, being made in human likeness. And being found in appearance as man, he humbled himself and became obedient to death—even death on a cross! (Phil. 2:6-8)

Paul tells us that Jesus, though being "in very nature God," "made himself nothing," "made [himself] in human likeness," "in the appearance of a man," "humbled himself," and even died. John does not give us a full explanation of the specifics of how Jesus did all of this. It's a mystery. What he does do is show us the life that Jesus lived, and how he lived it. That's John's best explanation.

The book of John is full of incredible Christology—the study of Christ. John could not be more direct in showing Jesus as God, his divinity. Consider the very first verses: "In the beginning was the Word, and the Word was with God, and the Word was God…The Word became flesh and made his dwelling among us" (John 1:1, 14). Clearly, the Word is God, and Jesus is the Word. Therefore, Jesus is God. John could not be more to the point.

There are also seven "I am" statements in John's book. The significance of these originates in the Old Testament account of Moses at the burning bush.

> Moses said to God, "Suppose I go to the Israelites and say to them, 'The God of your fathers has sent me to you,' and they ask me, 'What is his name?' Then what shall I tell them?" God said to Moses, "I AM WHO I AM. This is what you are to say to the

Israelites: 'I AM has sent me to you.'" (Ex. 3:13-14) "I am" is the name of God. The one who is, the preexistent one. So, when Jesus says, "I am," everyone in that culture knows he is claiming to be God. Here's an example from John 8. Jesus is in a discussion with the Pharisees, the Jewish religious leaders, talking about Abraham and their lineage.

> "Your father Abraham rejoiced at the thought of seeing my day; he saw it and was glad." "You are not yet fifty years old," the Jews said to him, "and you have seen Abraham!" "I tell you the truth," Jesus answered, "before Abraham was born, I am!" At this, they picked up stones to stone him... (John 8:56-59)

There was no doubt that day about what Jesus was claiming. He was claiming to be preexistent, before Abraham. He was claiming to be the "I AM," God himself. The Jews knew it, and they tried to kill him because of it. John is very adamant about communicating the fact that Jesus was God and that he claimed to be God in the flesh.

But it's critical to note that Jesus is also human. It's his humanity, after all, that gives me hope that I might be able to follow in his footsteps. But how was he both God and human? In Chapter 1, John starts dropping clues.

> He [John the Baptist] did not fail to confess, but confessed freely, "I am not the Christ." They asked him, "Then who are you? Are you Elijah?" He said, "I am not." "Are you the Prophet?" He answered, "No." (John 1:20-21)

Notice that they did not ask John the Baptist if he was "a" prophet. They asked, if he was "the" prophet. Who is the Prophet? A verses later, we read,

> Now some Pharisees who had been sent questioned

him, "Why then do you baptize if you are not the
Christ, or Elijah, nor the Prophet?" (John 1:24-25)
Notice the same thing. Who is "the" Prophet? There is no
written title anywhere in the Scriptures, other than here
in John, that gives reference to the Prophet.

Philip found Nathanael and told him, "We found
the one Moses wrote about in the Law, and about
whom the prophets also wrote—Jesus of Nazareth,
son of Joseph." (John 1:45)

When did Moses write about Jesus in the Law, the To-
rah, the first five books of the Bible? He didn't, at least
not specifically. You won't find the name Jesus anywhere
in these books. But these are clues designed to get you
thinking and wondering. Like when Jesus says to the
Jewish leaders,

"But do not think I will accuse you before the Father.
Your accuser is Moses, on whom your hopes are set.
If you believed Moses, you would believe me, for he
wrote about me. But since you do not believe what
he wrote, how are you going to believe what I say?"
(John 5:45-46)

Jesus says that Moses wrote about him. Yet there is no
reference to Jesus in Genesis, Exodus, Leviticus, Num-
bers, or Deuteronomy.

After the people saw the miraculous sign that Jesus
did, they began to say, "Surely this is the Prophet
who is to come into the world." (John 6:14)

John finally says it. Jesus is the Prophet.

So, let's follow the clues. If Jesus is the Prophet,
then the only place that Moses could be referring to him
is in Deuteronomy 18.

The Lord your God will raise up for you a prophet
like me from among your own brothers. You must

112

listen to him…I will raise up for them a prophet like you from among their brothers; I will put my words in his mouth, and he will tell them everything I command him. If anyone does not listen to my words that the prophet speaks in my name, I myself will call him to account. But a prophet who presumes to speak in my name anything I have not commanded him to say, or a prophet who speaks in the name of other gods, must be put to death. (Deut. 18:15, 18-20)

This description seems generic enough. It could be true for all prophets. But John is using this reference to say that it is especially true for Jesus, as the Prophet. It's a given that Jesus was a prophet. Why Deuteronomy 18 and the Prophet? Why does John make this reference so important? The answer is found in the Deuteronomy passage, and Moses says it twice. Notice where the Prophet will come from: "from among your brothers." The one defining characteristic of the Prophet is that he will be human. John uses Jesus' status as the Prophet to establish his humanity.

This will also be John's method for showing us how Jesus did it. What are the general characteristics of prophets?

1 They are sent by God.
2 They act as messengers for God.
3 They can't add anything to the message. They're teaching is not their own.
4 They are empowered by God, the Spirit. They can't do it in their own strength or initiative.
5 They must be obedient and dependent on God's leading. Their wills are yielded, surrendered or submissive to the will of God, who leads them.

113

Do some of these characteristics sound familiar? Hang on to them as we continue to walk through the book of John.

John not only tells us that Jesus is the Prophet, but he's also going to show us how Jesus lived out this title. After which, we'll see the words "follow me" in a whole new light. Ready? In the book of John, the word "sent" is used forty-one times in reference to Jesus' being sent by the Father. Note that God, comes and goes wherever he wants. He's God. But prophets are sent. They take orders. Let's walk chapter-by-chapter as John reveals to us the Prophet.

Chapter 3 John the Baptist says this about Jesus:

> The one [Jesus] who comes from above is above all; the one who is from the earth [John the Baptist] belongs to the earth, and speaks as one from the earth. The one who comes from heaven is above all. He testifies to what he has seen and heard, but no one accepts his testimony. The man who has accepted it has certified that God is truthful. For the one whom God has sent speaks the words of God, for God gives the Spirit without limit.
> (John 3:31-34)

Jesus is sent to speak the words of God. He is the Prophet. Chapter 4 John records,

> "My food," said Jesus, "is to do the will of him who sent me and to finish his work." (John 4:34)

These words are clearly spoken from a God who has, in some form, emptied himself of being equal to the I AM and has become human, a prophet. Jesus is sent, and his will is submissive to the Father's.

Chapter 5

> Jesus gave them this answer: "I tell you the truth,

> the Son can do nothing by himself; he can do only what he sees his Father doing, because whatever the Father does the Son also does." (John 5:19)

Notice: The son can do nothing by himself. He can't initiate. Humility requires that he not do it on his own. He has to be led and empowered.

> "By myself I can do nothing; I judge only as I hear, and my judgement is just, for I seek not to please myself but him who sent me." (John 5:30)

This admission—"By myself I can do nothing"—communicates that Jesus is totally dependent. By himself, he can't do miracles. By himself, he can't cast out demons. By himself, he can't speak for God the Father. He has emptied himself and has become just like you and me. He is fully human. In these verses he is supernaturally empowered by the Spirit, and he is sent. The word "sent" is used five times in Chapter 5 alone.

Chapter 6

> "For I have come down from heaven not to do my will but to do the will of him who sent me. And this is the will of him who sent me, that I shall lose none of all that he has given me, but raise them up at the last day." (John 6:38-39)

Jesus' will is yielded to his Father's, and he is sent. "Sent" is also used five times in this chapter.

Chapter 7

> Jesus answered, "My teaching is not my own. It comes from him who sent me. If anyone chooses to do God's will, he will find out whether my teaching comes from God or whether I speak on my own. He who speaks on his own does so to gain honor for himself, but he who works for the honor of the one who sent him is a man of truth; there is nothing false

about him." (John 7:16-18)

In this passage we see that Jesus is sent. The phrase "works for the honor of" shows that his submissive will is surrendered to his Father's. Jesus' claim that his "teaching is not [his] own" prompts the question, Why can't Jesus, the God of all creation, have his own teaching? The answer is that he can, and he does, unless he's playing the humble role of the Prophet here on earth. In that case, something has to give. So, Jesus gave up, emptied himself of the right to his own teaching, somehow without giving up any of his own divinity. And he did it so that he could look us in the eye and say, "I didn't cheat; I became just like you."

Later in Chapter 7, John reports,

> Then Jesus, still teaching in the temple courts, cried out, "Yes, you know me, and you know where I am from. I am not here on my own, but he who sent me is true. You do not know him, but I know him because I am from him and he sent me."
> (John 7:28-29)

Jesus, the Prophet, is "sent."

Chapter 8 John gives us this picture:

> "I have much to say in judgment of you. But he who sent me is reliable, and what I have heard from him I tell the world." They did not understand that he was telling them about his Father. So Jesus said, "When you have lifted up the Son of Man, then you will know that I am the one I claim to be and that I do nothing on my own but speak just what the Father has taught me. The one who sent me is with me; he has not left me alone, for I always do what pleases him." (John 8:26-29)

This passage shows that Jesus is "sent," that he would "always do what pleases" the Father, and that "he does nothing on his own." In all that he does, Jesus is led and empowered by the Father. Stop and think for a second. In Luke 7:11-17, when Jesus raises the widow's son at Nain, how did he do it? Being God, did he just speak on his own initiative, out of his own power, and the boy rose from the grave? Did he do it because he wanted to, because he was God and he could? Or did it happened because the Father showed compassion for a woman who had lost her only son? And that same compassion moved in and through Jesus. Then the Father led him, empowered him, and worked the miracle through Jesus. The synoptics tell us who, what, and where. But they don't tell us how. Later on in Chapter 8, Jesus says,

> "I am telling you what I have seen in the Father's presence, and you do what you have heard from your Father." "Abraham is our father," they answered. "If you were Abraham's children," said Jesus, "then you would do the things Abraham did. As it is, you are determined to kill me, a man who has told you the truth that I heard from God."
> (John 8:38-40)

Jesus, a messenger, is telling them what he has "heard from God."

> "...I honor my Father and you dishonor me. I am not seeking glory for myself; but there is one who seeks it, and he is the judge...Though you do not know him, I know him. If I said I did not, I would be a liar like you, but I do know him and keep his word." (John 8:49-50, 55)

Jesus, as the Prophet, obediently honors his Father by seeking his glory and keeping his word. Five times in Chapter 8 the word "sent" is used in reference to Jesus. Chapter 9 The man born blind says this about Jesus:

"We know that God does not listen to sinners. He listens to the godly man who does his will. Nobody has ever heard of opening the eyes of a man born blind. If this man were not from God, he could do nothing." (John 9:31-33)

Jesus is from God. He does God's will. And he can heal blindness because he is enabled and empowered by the Father.

Chapter 10 John again quotes Jesus:

"What about the one whom the Father set apart as his very own and sent into the world? Why then do you accuse me of blasphemy because I said, 'I am God's Son?' Do not believe me unless I do what my Father does. But if I do it, even though you do not believe me, believe the miracles, that you may know and understand that the Father is in me, and I am in the Father." (John 10:36-38)

Jesus says that he is "set apart" and sent. He says that he does what his Father does, that the Father leads him in all that he does. He says that he is united with the Father and that the Father is in him, empowering him. The pages of the book of John drip with the idea of Jesus as the Prophet.

Chapter 12

"Now my heart is troubled, and what shall I say? 'Father, save me from this hour'? No, it was for this very reason I came to this hour. Father, glorify your name!" (John 12:27-28)

Jesus' will, like a prophet's, is submissive to that of the Father's, even to the point of death.

Then Jesus cried out, "When a man believes in me, he does not believe in me only, but in the one who sent me. When he looks at me, he sees the one who sent me." (John 12:44-45)

Jesus, the Prophet, is sent, and though he is fully human as a prophet, he is also fully God. He is both emptied and, at the same time, has all of "the fullness of God" in him. It's a mystery.

> "For I did not speak of my own accord, but the Father who sent me commanded me what to say and how to say it. I know that his command leads to eternal life. So whatever I say is just what the Father has told me to say." (John 12:49-50)

It couldn't be any more clear: Jesus is the Prophet. He didn't speak on his own accord, by his own initiative, or through his own teaching. The Father told him what to say. The Father told him how to say it. And the Father empowered him to be able to say it.

I love the intimacy displayed in John 13-17. These chapters detail the disciples' last night with Jesus before the crucifixion. He shares with them all the important things they need to know before he leaves. In Chapter 14, he twice stops in the middle of what he's telling them and says, "The words I say to you are not just my own" (14:10), and "These words you hear are not my own; they belong to the Father who sent me" (14:24). Even in simple conversation with the disciples, the Father is leading him, and Jesus knows it. And because he has pointed it out, he wants the disciples (and you and me) to know it as well.

Why is this so important? It's absolutely crucial! It's crucial because Jesus is not inviting us to a life he hasn't lived. He came for the sake of God's holy name. He did battle as God in order to win us back. As God, he invites us to the unseen realm—his realm, his kingdom. And we can only enter and function there by a dependent faith in a God who can deliver. As God, he washed us, took away our old hearts, gave us new ones, and he has indwelled us. But the life he wants to give us could not be demonstrated with just words, by just talking about it. The life had to be lived. The only way to show us, the only way to model it for us, was to become the Prophet. He had to become God incarnate, to take on flesh and become like you and me. Jesus can now say, "I know exactly how you feel and what you're thinking. I've been there." This means we have a high priest who can empathize with us.

> For we do not have a high priest who is unable to sympathize with our weaknesses, but we have one who has been tempted in every way, just as we are—yet was without sin. (Heb. 4:15)

Now, when Jesus says "follow me," we hear his invitation in a whole new way. We hear it in the correct context. God wants to do something through me. Just like he did with Jesus. Jesus shows me what following looks like. Before, it was the Ronnie show, me trying my hardest to look and become like Jesus, sinless. And left to myself, my old heart, my own power, it looked like Israel in the Old Testament trying to keep the law. It wasn't pretty. But Jesus invites me to a dependent trust or gaze upon him, in the same way he did with the Father. He invites me, in the same way, to be empowered by him, just like he was empowered by the Father. He invites me to be led, in the same way, to let him work through me, just like the Father did with Jesus. And, last but by no means least, he invites me, in the same way, to an intimacy that is beyond my wildest dreams. Folks, there is more. There is always more with God.

11
In The Same Way

The pyramid is now full. It's complete. But it's been transformed from a pyramid to a pile of rocks. It has become ten smooth stones, an altar by my river Jordan (Josh. 4:1-9). They stand as a reminder of what God has done in my life. They're a reminder of how he's made his name holy, through us, before their eyes. It's a visual reminder of the life Jesus invites us to, a life that we can't imagine or comprehend. It's beyond our wildest dreams.

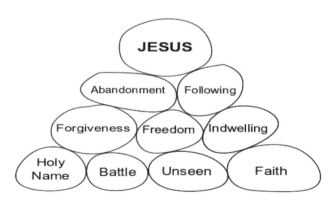

You might be confused at this point. Up to now, I've articulated a life in which you've been bought. You are a slave, and your life is not your own. Your slavery has been transferred from the enemy over to God. And this is a life so great that it's unimaginable? Yes, it is! You've been invited to yield, surrender, abandon, and die. And now you're supposed to follow Jesus. You're being asked to let yourself be led to what looks like the same martyr's death that Jesus died. Yes, that's it! Life beyond your wildest dreams! In truth, it's not what you thought, is it?

It's the life of Jesus. And it's a life that's hidden from the seen realm. It makes no sense to the outside world. It's covered in paradox.

"For whoever wants to save his life will lose it, but whoever loses his life for me will save it."(Luke 9:24)

"Whoever finds his life will lose it, and whoever loses his life for my sake will find it." (Matt. 10:39)

Jesus said, "For judgment I have come into this world, so that the blind will see and those who see will become blind." (John 9:39)

For the message of the cross is foolishness to those who are perishing, but to us who are being saved it is the power of God.

For the foolishness of God is wiser than man's wisdom, and the weakness of God is stronger than man's strength.

But God chose the foolish things of the world to shame the wise; God chose the weak things of the world to shame the strong. He chose the lowly things of this world and the despised things—and the things that are not—to nullify the things that are, so that no one may boast before him.
(1 Cor. 1:18, 25, 27-29)

God has hidden this life from the outside, seen world. You can't steal it or take it by force; it must be given. You can't figure it out; it must be revealed. You can't live it in your own strength; you must be empowered. God, not us, will make his name holy. But once you've found this life, once you've tasted it, it's like a pearl.

The kingdom of heaven is like a treasure hidden in a field. When a man found it, he hid it again, and then in his joy went and sold all he had and bought that field. Again, the kingdom of heaven is like a merchant looking for fine pearls. When he found one of great value, he went away and sold everything he had and bought it. (Matt. 13:44-45)

The next time you get the chance, listen to some old person give their testimony. These will be people who have given their lives to Christ and have spent years suffering all the things we've talked about. They've surrendered and yielded and obeyed and followed and lost everything for the sake of knowing Christ Jesus. They've lived the life of Jesus. Stop and listen to them. Listen hard for any indications of regret. I guarantee you won't hear any. In fact, I bet it'll almost sound like they are inviting you to share in a treasure they've found.

All that Christ does is covered in paradox. Jesus comes to do battle and is going to defeat the evil one... by dying—by dying the death of a common criminal on a cross. It is paradox. And he invites you to this same paradox. The root of the enemy's fall was pride. He sold Adam and Eve on this same pride. And you and I, in all our independence and sin, have bought in and immersed ourselves in this same subtle pride. So, when God sends Jesus to defeat the enemy, sin and pride, should it surprise us that humility is the central weapon with which he does battle? Listen again to how Murray describes this plan of humility. It surprised me when I first read it.

> ...the relation of the creature to God could only be one of unceasing, absolute, universal dependence....Humility, the place of entire dependence on God, is, from the very

nature of things, the first duty and the highest virtue of the creature. In fact, it is the root of every virtue…[1]

What we saw in the Prophet was humility—a constant dependence on the presence, power, enablement, and leading from the Father. Murray goes on,

> Our one need is to study and know and trust the life that has been revealed in Christ as the life that is now ours, and waits for our consent to gain possession and mastery of our whole being. In this view it is of inconceivable importance that we should have right thoughts of what Christ is—of what really constitutes Him the Christ—and specially of what may be counted His chief characteristic, the root and essence of all His character as our Redeemer. There can be but one answer: it is His humility. What is the incarnation but His heavenly humility, His emptying Himself and becoming man? What is His life on earth but humility, His taking the form of a servant? And what is His atonement but humility? "He humbled Himself and became obedient unto death." And what is His ascension and His glory but humility exalted to the throne and crowned with glory? "He humbled Himself, therefore God highly exalted Him." In heaven where He was with the Father, in His birth, in His life, in His death, in His sitting on the throne, it is all—it is nothing but humility. Christ is the humility of God embodied in human nature…If this be the root of the tree, its nature must be seen in every branch and leaf and fruit. If humility be the first, the all-including grace of the life of Jesus—if humility be the secret of His atonement—then the health and strength of our spiritual life will entirely depend upon our putting this grace first also, and making humility the chief thing we admire in Him, the chief thing we ask of Him, the one thing for which we sacrifice all else.[2]

The life he invites us to is characterized by humility and dependence. It's the same humility that defeated the enemy at the cross. Remember, God is the one at work.

He is doing something incredibly humble yet powerful through us for the sake of his holy name. All he requires is faith, dependence, humility. They are all of the same essence.

The key to this life, this pearl, this treasure, is how Jesus gives it. He wraps it in an intimacy that is beyond our imaginations. He invites us in. He invites us in to him. He unites himself with us. We have already seen this in the gospel. We have seen how Christ takes away our old hearts, our old selves, by pinning them to the cross, within himself. This union is not just functional with regard to our redemption. It is also the basis of our life together.

Paul's favorite phrase throughout his epistles is "In Christ." It's how he describes this union, the source of life. Listen to how Paul articulates it over and over again.

–buried with him in baptism (Rom. 6:4; Col. 2:12)
–we have been crucified with Christ (Rom. 6:6; Gal. 2:20)
–we count ourselves dead to sin and alive to God in Christ (Rom. 6:11)
–we have been raised with him (Col. 2:12, 3:1; Eph. 2:6)
–the free gift of God is eternal life in Christ (Rom. 6:23)
–there is no condemnation for those in Christ (Rom. 8:1)
–we are co-heirs with Christ (Rom. 8:17; Gal. 3:29)
–nothing can separate us from the love of God that is in Christ (Rom. 8:39)
–many form one body in Christ (Rom. 12:4)
–we are sanctified in Christ (1 Cor. 1:2)
–grace is given to us in Christ (1 Cor. 1:4; 2 Tim. 1:9)
–we are wise in Christ (1 Cor. 4:10)
–we have 10,000 guardians in Christ (1 Cor. 4:15)
–we have hope in Christ (1 Cor. 15:19)
–God makes us stand firm in Christ (2 Cor 1:21)
–God always leads us in triumphal procession in Christ (2 Cor. 2:14)
–in Christ we speak like men sent from God (2 Cor. 2:17)
–confidence is ours through Christ (2 Cor. 3:4)
–the veil is removed from our eyes in Christ (2 Cor. 3:14)
–we are new creations in Christ (2 Cor. 5:17)

–we've been reconciled through Christ (2 Cor. 5:18-19)
–freedom we have in Christ (Gal. 2:4)
–justified in Christ (Gal. 2:17)
–clothed with Christ (Gal. 3:27)
–we are all one in Christ (Gal. 3:28)
–blessed with every spiritual blessing in Christ (Eph. 1:3)
–God chose us in him (Christ) (Eph. 1:4, 11)
–adopted as sons through Christ (Eph. 1:5)
–glorious grace freely given in Christ (Eph. 1:6)
–in him we have redemption through his blood (Eph. 1:7)
–knowledge of the mystery of his will, purposed in Christ
     (Eph. 1:9)
–you were included in Christ (Eph. 1:13)
–he seated us with him in the heavenly realm in Christ
     (Eph. 2:6)
–created in Christ (Eph. 2:10)
–in Christ we have been brought near (Eph. 2:13)
–his eternal purpose was accomplished in Christ
     (Eph. 3:11)
–in him we may approach God with freedom and
     confidence (Eph. 3:12)
–fruit of righteousness came through Christ (Phil. 1:11)
–joy in Christ (Phil. 1:26)
–God called me heavenward in Christ (Phil. 3:14)
–peace of God which transcends all understanding, will
     guard your hearts and minds in Christ (Phil. 4:7)
–God will meet all your needs according to his glorious
     riches in Christ (Phil. 4:19)
–in Christ all the fullness of Deity lives in bodily form
     and you have been given fullness in Christ
     (Col. 2:9-10)
–in him you were circumcised (Col. 2:11)
–made alive with Christ (Col. 2:13)
–died with Christ to the basic principles of the world
     (Col. 2:20)
–died and your life is hidden with Christ in God
     (Col. 3:3)
–the dead in Christ will rise first (1 Thess. 4:16)
–be joyful always, pray continually, give thanks in all cir-
     cumstances, for this is God's will for you in Christ
     (1 Thess. 5:16-18)
–the grace of our Lord was poured out on me abundantly,

along with the faith and love that are in Christ
  (1 Tim. 1:14)
–faith and love that are in Christ (1 Tim. 1:14; 2 Tim. 1:13)
–the promise of life that is in Christ (2 Tim. 1:1)
–be strong in grace that is in Christ (2 Tim. 2:1)
–salvation that is in Christ (2 Tim. 2:10)
–every good thing we have in Christ (Philemon 1:6)

I've listed all of these verses so that you could get a sense of the fullness of this union. It is the center of our life with Christ. To be a follower of Jesus is to live "in him." Chafer writes,

> Our baptism into Jesus Christ can be none other than the act of God in placing us in Christ (Galatians 3:27)… The argument in this passage is based on this vital union by which we are organically united to Christ though our baptism into His body…Being baptized into Jesus Christ is the substance of which co-crucifixion, co-death, co-burial and co-resurrection are attributes. One is the cause: while the others are the effects. All this is unto the realization of one great divine purpose. "That like as Christ was raised up from the dead by the glory of the Father, even so we also should walk in newness of life," or by a new life principle. Our "walk," then, is the divine objective.[3]

This life in Christ has already been defined. It is a life of humility, dependence, dying to self, following, being attentive. It's also a life united in some special, crazy way with the God of the Universe.

On the night before his crucifixion, Jesus describes this intimate connection to his disciples:

Remain in me, and I will remain in you. No branch can bear fruit by itself; it must remain in the vine. Neither can you bear fruit unless you remain in me. I am the vine; you are the branches. If a man remains in me and I in him, he will bear much fruit;

apart from me you can do nothing. (John 15:4-5) Jesus invites us to remain, to stay connected—other translations say "to abide." This is the secret. Thomas Kelly writes,

> But, more deeply, He who is within us urges, by secret persuasion, to such an amazing Inward Life with Him, so that, firmly cleaving to Him, we always look out upon all the world through the sheen of the Inward Light, and react towards men spontaneously and joyously from this Inward Center. Yield yourself to Him who is a far better teacher than these outward words, and you will have found the Instructor Himself, of whom these words are a faint and broken echo. Such practice of inward orientation, of inward worship and listening, is no mere counsel for special religious groups, for small religious orders, for special "interior souls," for monks retired in cloisters. This practice is the heart of religion. It is the secret, I am persuaded, of the inner life of the Master of Galilee. He expected this secret to be freshly discovered in everyone who would be his follower...It lies in that call to all men to the practice of orienting their entire being in inward adoration about the springs of immediacy and ever fresh divine power within the secret silences of the soul. The Inner Light, the Inward Christ, is no mere doctrine, belonging peculiarly to a small religious fellowship, to be accepted or rejected as a mere belief. It is the living Center of Reference for all Christian souls.[4]

There is a life in Christ that the enemy does not want you to know exists. It is a life in the unseen realm. And it is a life of dependent faith and humility. The saints of old simply referred to it as "union."

I get one last shot, a final attempt, to present to you this life beyond your wildest dreams. When you were a teenager and getting ready to leave the house on a Friday night, your parents probably gave you some last-minute instructions before you walked out the door.

Let's say your mom or dad gave you the same directive ten different times in ten different ways. Ten times means it must be something very, very important. It's a "your life depends on it" kind of importance.

Well, ten times in his book John records Jesus saying virtually the same thing, drawing a verbal parallel. And eight of the ten times are communicated on Jesus' last night with the disciples (John 13-17). Eight times in one evening. Here it is, your life depends on it. The first time occurs in John 6, and it's a small introduction.

> (1) Just as the living Father sent me and I live because of the Father, so the one who feeds on me will live because of me. (John 6:57)

In other words, Jesus lives because of the Father. In the same way, we live because of Jesus.

This idea is repeated a little differently in John 10.

> (2) I am the good shepherd; I know my sheep and my sheep know me—just as the Father knows me and I know the Father—and I lay down my life for the sheep. (John 10:14-15)

Jesus knows his sheep and his sheep know him, in the same way that the Father knows Jesus and Jesus knows the Father. The key here is just as or in the same way. As we enter John's account of Jesus' last night, I'm going to quit the commentary and simply let you observe the verbal parallel in the following verses. I have added (in the same way) for emphasis.

(3) I tell you the truth, whoever accepts anyone I send accepts me; and (in the same way) whoever accepts me accepts the one who sent me. (John 13:20)

(4) On that day you will realize that I am in my Father, and you are in me, and (in the same way) I am in you. (John 14:20)

Notice: these next two verses are one right after another.

(5) As the Father has loved me, (in the same way) so have I loved you. Now remain in my love. (John 15:9)

(6) If you obey my commands, you will remain in my love, just as I have obeyed my Father's commands and remain in his love. (John 15:10)

These next three are in Jesus' high priestly prayer in John 17, in which he is talking to the Father.

(7) As you sent me [Jesus] into the world, (in the same way) I have sent them into the world. (John 17:18)

(8) I have given them the glory (in the same way) that you [the Father] gave me, that they may be one as (in the same way) we are one. (John 17:22)

(9) I [Jesus] in them and (in the same way) you [the Father] in me. May they be brought to complete unity to let the world know that you sent me and have loved them even as you have loved me. (John 17:23)

And finally, after the resurrection, Jesus appears to the disciples.

(10) Again Jesus said, "Peace be with you! As the Father sent me, (in the same way) I am sending

you. (John 20:21)

The Trinity—Jesus and the Father and the Holy Spirit—is the mother of all relationships. This is the primal source of our understanding of relationship. How would you rate the relationship between God the Father and God the Son? On a scale of one to ten, it's an eleven. Here is John's point: Jesus wants, in the same way, the same kind of relationship with you that he has with the Father. He invites you, in the same way, to the same love, the same presence, the same empowerment and enablement, the same voice, and the same words. It goes on and on. He invites you, in the same way, to the same life that he lived, indwelled by the Father. Only, Jesus is indwelling you.

When Jesus the Prophet spoke, God spoke through him.

> For I did not speak of my own accord, but the Father who sent me commanded me what to say and how to say it. (John 12:49)

And *in the same way,*

> On my account you will be brought before governors and kings as witnesses to them and to the Gentiles. But when they arrest you, do not worry about what to say or how to say it. At that time you will be given what to say, for it will not be you speaking, but the Spirit of your Father speaking through you. (Matt. 10:18-20)

Three times Jesus says, "I do nothing on my own" (John 5:19, 30; 8:28).

> Jesus said, "When you have lifted up the Son of Man, then you will know that I am the one I claim to be and that I do nothing on my own but speak just what the Father has taught me." (John 8:28)

131

In the same way, he says this about you and me:
> I am the vine; you are the branches. If a man re-
> mains in me and I in him, he will bear much fruit;
> apart from me you can do nothing. (John 15:5)

Jesus invites you and me to the life he lived, in the same way. He invites us to live it just like he did. He didn't cheat. He came and modeled it for us. For three years he walked in front of the disciples in dependent humility with the Father, and then on the last night, he told them to live their lives in the same way. But more than that, in a much deeper way, Jesus wants to continue living his life through us. It's not just our life you see, but in some crazy way it's his as well. And His life is a life beyond your wildest dreams. Tozer would say it's the life of a prophet.

> Hearts that are "fit to break" with love for the Godhead are those who have been in the Presence and have looked with opened eye upon the majesty of Deity. Men of the breaking hearts had a quality about them not known to or understood by common men. They habitually spoke with spiritual authority. They had been in the Presence of God and they reported what they saw there. They were prophets, not scribes, for the scribe tells us what he has read, and the prophet tells what he has seen. The distinction is not an imaginary one. Between the scribe who has read and the prophet who has seen there is a difference as wide as the sea. We are today overrun with orthodox scribes, but the prophets, where are they? The hard voice of the scribe sounds over evangelicalism, but the Church waits for the tender voice of the saint who has penetrated the veil and has gazed with inward eye upon the Wonder that is God. And yet, thus to pene-trate, to push in sensitive living experience into the holy Presence, is a privilege open to every child of God.[5]

The summons is here. The bell has been rung, and the invitation goes forth. It's a call to a life you can't imag-ine. It's a life found only in Christ, and the invitation is open to "every child of God." The paradox, the secret, is that only the hungry long for it, only the blind can see it, and only the desperate can hear it. It's an invitation to life, in the same way, the same way Jesus did with the Father. And His life, in you and through you, is a life beyond your wildest dreams.

Acknowledgments

Some brief thank-yous are in order. Thank you to my wife, Sharon, who transcribed 180 pages of handwritten scribbling onto a laptop and walked with me through the entire project. Her finger print is on every page and this book is as much hers as it is mine. She has endured 33 years of marriage with me, and her passion for Christ continues to inspire me. She is the most godly woman I know. Thank you to Nathan and Samuel, my two sons, who have been the delight of my life and who have taught me so much about the love of the Father. Nathan designed the cover and did the formatting. Samuel read the entire book to me out loud as the last edit. Thank you to Peggy Howard for her early editing expertise, to Aaron Wedemeyer for giving the text its final form, and to Michael Manes for getting everything camera ready. These folks have been partners in ministry over the years, and the book you hold would not be the same without them. Thank you to my sweet sister Lori, the Brittain's, Rush's and Goen's. They are the only family I have left. Thank you to Neal Howard, Kevin Sparks and the "Lake Clan" for befriending me for thirty years, pushing me to follow Jesus and being just like family. Thank you to Howard Baker for investing in me, John Clifford for believing in me and Joe Warren for teaching me grace. Thank you to the ATF pastors and Ruidosa Boys for including me. Thank you to Chris and Margret Lemon for sharing life with us in Waco and their son Josh Lemon for the illustrations and great triangles. Thank you to Jed Walker and P. Michael Smith for meeting with me most Mondays and keeping me straight. Thank you to Barry and Nancy Beal, the entire Sparks family, and a whole slew of Midland folks who, for years, have embraced us and our calling. And for all the many more unnamed others who have done the same. There are not enough thank-yous for all that each of you have done. Thank you to Young Life for allowing me to serve as a volunteer and staff member. It was in the midst of ministry that I grew up and all of these ideas took form. Thank you to all the Young Life staff, my friends, who have allowed me over the years to steal their stuff and now call it my own. Thank you to all my Young Life high school and college friends, voluteer leaders and committee who over the years have allowed me into their lives and continue to love me. It is an incredible privilege. Thank you to the Home Builders II Sunday school class for allowing me to teach and develop these thoughts in the midst of many years of life together. Thank you to all the folks who have endured one of my spiritual retreats as I have slowly put together much of this material. Thank you to all the people I presently meet with as a spiritual director and coach. All of you have shaped and impacted me and this book in so many ways. Thank you! Thank you! Thank you!

Notes

All Scripture quotations are taken from The Holy Bible, New International Version. Copyright © 1973, 1978, 1984 by International Bible Society

Chapter 1
1. George MacDonald, The Curate's Awakening (Minneapolis: Bethany House, 1985), 80-81.
2. Ibid., 177.
3. A.W. Tozer, The Pursuit of God (Harrisburg, PA: Christian Publications, 1948), 11-12.
4. Eugene H. Peterson, Working the Angles: The Shape of Pastoral Integrity (Grand Rapids: Eerdmans, 1987), 32-33.

Chapter 2
1. Andrew Murray, Humility (Fort Washington, PA: CLC Publications, 1997), 13.

Chapter 3
1. Tozer, 56.

Chapter 4
1. Tozer, 86.
2. Murray, 72-73.

136

3. Jean-Pierre De Caussade, The Sacrament of the Present Moment (San Francisco: Harper, 1989), 103.
4. Lewis Sperry Chafer, He That is Spiritual (Grand Rapids: Zondervan, 1967), 45-46.
5. Tozer, 89.
6. Ibid., 90.
7. Ibid., 91-92.

Chapter 5
1. Chafer, 74-75.
2. Miles J Stanford, The Green Letters (Grand Rapids: Zondervan, 1975), 18-20.
3. MacDonald, 176.

Chapter 6
1. Chafer, 60.
2. Murray, (Like Christ, p. 176), The Green Letters, p.44
3. Watchman Nee, (The Normal Christian Life, p.25), The Green Letters, p.45
4. Stanford, 64-65.
5. Chafer, 121.

Chapter 7
1. Robert E. Colman, The Master Plan of Evangelism (Old Tappan, NJ: Revell Company, 1963), 66-67.
2. Brother Lawrence, The Practice of the Presence of God (Grand Rapids: Baker Book House, 1958), 19.
3. Colman, 69-70.
4. Chafer, 52, 61.
5. Ibid., 55.
6. Ibid., 58.

Chapter 8
1. G.K. Chesterton, What's Wrong with the World
2. Murray, 77-79, 81-83.
3. Tozer, 23.
4. Ibid., 26-27, 30-31.
5. De Caussade, 10, 28, 49-50.
6. Ibid., 70-71.
7. Thomas R. Kelly, The Testament of Devotion (San Francisco: Harper, 1941), 43-44.

Chapter 9
1. Chafer, 87.
2. De Caussade, 98-99.
3. MacDonald, 83.
4. Tozer, 66-67, 71.

Chapter 11
1. Murray, 12-13.
2. Ibid., 20-21.
3. Chafer, 122-123.
4. Kelly, 6, 8.
5. Tozer, 42-43.

Discussion Questions

Chapter 1

1. What has taken center stage in your story this past week?

2. If someone were to look at your life—your schedule of activities—whose name would they say is being promoted?

3. God wanted to repair the damage Israel had done to his name. He chose Israel, the party that had caused the damage, to be the medium he would use to repair it. In what ways have you damaged God's holy name? How is your transformation being used to repair it? What does it say about God that he chose to use you in this process?

4. How does the idea that prayer is answering speech impact how you pray?

5. How might the thought, it is now and has always been God doing the work, change the way you live out your calling?

6. If showing God's name to be holy was the most important thing in our lives, how would tomorrow, or this next week, look different?

Chapter 2

1. What areas of insecurity in your life are easily attacked by the enemy? (He commonly targets our bodies, our identity, and our purpose.)

2. In what ways are you slow to depend upon the Lord and why? Who or what are you depending on instead of Christ?

3. What areas of pride are a struggle for you?

4. How does the reality of spiritual battle impact your time with Jesus in the morning? How does it impact your walk with him during the day?

5. How do you mentally connect the act of prayer with joining Christ in the battle?

6. When you are being tempted, do you see the temptation as an opportunity to sin (to get what you want), or as an opportunity for independence (to be in control), or as an invitation from God to depend on him?

Chapter 3

1. How did your seen world realities swallow you up or demand your attention yesterday? This past week?

2. What unseen world realities do you struggle to keep? Which one is the hardest for you?

3. Where in your life is the Lord asking you to step into the unseen realm, to step into faith?

4. What are the imminent dangers of overlooking the unseen world?

5. Though invisible, this unseen world is neither imagined nor fantasy. In what ways is it real?

6. How does the reality of an unseen realm challenge your paradigms?

7. What new truth has Jesus invited you to believe? What is your plan to make it a reality in your life?

Chapter 4

1. How would you define faith? Where have you seen it?

2. Would you say your life is based on performance, works, and rules? Are you satisfied with your life? Do you long for a better one?

3. If you were listed as one of the "heroes of the faith," why would you have earned this title? What has been your most significant act of faith so far?

4. Where is your gaze directed? How is that gaze impacting your life?

5. Why do you think that faith, of all things, is what pleases God the most?

6. What is God inviting you to believe about him or trust him with today?

7. How has your paradigm changed in terms of what God wants and expects from you?

Chapter 5

1. Why is it that we tend to trust in our good works for God's acceptance?

2. Do you live your life as though your sins—past, present, and future—are completely gone, erased?

3. How would your life look different if you believed you were truly forgiven? How should Christ's love for us change the way we respond, act, and live?

4. Jesus is inviting you into a relationship in which you are his adopted brother/sister, in which you share in all that he inherits. The Father sees you as an adopted son/daughter. How should being in the family change how you live today?

5. Are you His Favorite? If God gave you a name that reflected how he felt about you, what would it be?

6. Can you think of a time when you were guilty of a wrong but the other person extended you forgiveness? What was this experience like for you? Can you think of a time when you extended forgiveness toward another person who had hurt you deeply? Why did you forgive? How did extending forgiveness affect you?

Chapter 6
1. What areas or things in your life do you need/want to be released or set free from?
2. What does it mean when the Scriptures say that your old heart is dead, considering that it is somehow still with you?
3. What are examples in your own life of old heart living or slavery? What are examples in your own life of living out of a new heart or freedom?
4. In what ways do you try to fix your old heart?
5. How is being crucified with Christ different from being forgiven by God? What has happened as a result of dying, of being buried and raised with Christ?
6. How does the concept of having two hearts help you understand what Christ is inviting you to? How does the paradigm of living out of one heart hinder you from experiencing what Christ has for you?
7. How could you practice living out of your new heart this next week?

Chapter 7
1. A. B. Simpson says that on our best days we are simply containers carrying Jesus. If that is true, what does it say about our role as members of the body of Christ? How does this relate to the concept of being sent?
2. Which of the Holy Spirit's roles—power, guidance and

intimacy—are you most familiar with? Which are you least familiar with?

3. Name some distractions that keep you from being attentive to the Spirit inside you. What did that inattentiveness look like yesterday? Last week?

4. Do you guide and dictate what your day will look like or does the Spirit? What do you think life being led by the Spirit should look like? How would it occur? What would happen in a normal day?

5. What makes living in the Spirit so hard for us? (There are multiple answers.)

6. How do you handle intimacy? What do you wish for your relationship with Jesus, as far as intimacy is concerned?

Chapter 8

1. What are the lies and distractions the enemy uses to keep you set in your old ways, your old patterns, your old heart?

2. What possesses your heart? What in your life gets the most time, attention, love, emotion, energy?

3. Be honest! What is your first response to these words: abandon, surrender, dying to self, yielded? What would Jesus say about them?

4. Is it surprising that, when Jesus says follow me, dying to ourselves would then be central to the life he is offering? Pick one area in your life, and tomorrow die to yourself in that area. How are your two hearts feeling about just the thought of doing that? Any surprises?

5. How do you put on or clothe yourself with your new heart? What would you do differently? What does that intentionality look like for you tomorrow? This next week?

6. What's your dream? Stop, think about it; dream a little.

Does it surprise you that God has a better one for you? Are you willing to kill yours on the altar in order to embrace his?

Chapter 9

1. What have you heard Jesus telling you to do today, and have you done it? How would this question change your time with him in the morning?

2. How might you acquire a lifelong habit of spiritual receptivity? How is Jesus inviting you to practice attentiveness this next week?

3. What keeps you from being attentive hourly to the Lord? What would it look like to practice something that allows you to be better at this?

4. Do you find yourself being led by Jesus or being oblivious to him? What's your plan for moving more toward being led?

5. Are you letting Jesus carry the load or are you doing all the work? What's he really asking from you and how do you remind yourself of that?

6. Have you ever experienced Jesus getting your attention? How is freely, actively, and intentionally offering Jesus your attention different from your present way of living? What does this difference call you to?

7. Does your heart long for more? Do you turn to God in earnestness? How would God draw you to hunger?

Chapter 10

1. What is your sense of being sent? How does being sent impact your experience of Jesus?

2. Have you, as a prophet, relayed a message for the Lord this week? He isn't asking you to create the message, just to pass it on. What was the message?

3. If the Father empowered Jesus to do everything he sent him to do, would not Jesus empower you to do everything he is asking you to do? What fears are presently holding you back from this experience?

4. Has the Lord asked you to do something recently? Have you responded in obedience by doing it?

5. How does being led differ from following? In what ways would you need to be intentional in order to make either happen?

6. Life beyond your wildest dreams is just beyond your sense of surrender and abandonment, of life not belonging to you, of being sent. Jesus knew this and lived this life for us. What stops you from following him? What keeps you from this life?

7. How does the life of Jesus being led by the Father change your paradigms? What is Jesus wanting, asking, and inviting you to?

Chapter 11

1. What is the opposite of pride? What do you think of Andrew Murray's connection of humility to dependence?

2. Why is paradox so powerful?

3. What's the difference between trying to be humble and wearing Jesus' humility? Is being in Christ something related to what we do or what we believe? How do your answers to those two questions impact your life each day?

4. Which of the many *in Christ* verses listed spoke to you most deeply and why?

5. How do you define the concept of abiding? Since the Spirit resides inside you, how do you pay attention to this inner presence? How does a person practice getting better at either one of these? What's your plan for doing this next week?

6. How is the intimacy being offered by Christ central to all that he is inviting us to? What does it say about God's Holy Name?

7. Do you really believe that you can live your life in the same way that Jesus did? How does the idea of in the same way challenge your paradigms?

8. How would you describe the life that Jesus is inviting us to? What's the first step towards living it?

About the Author and the Book

R. A. Smith is presently the director of Polwarth Ministries which has a focus on spiritual direction and leading retreats. For more information about either the author or the book check the website at:

polwarthministries.com